Mark Booth

Camp

QUARTET BOOKS

LONDON   MELBOURNE   NEW YORK

First published by Quartet Books Limited 1983
A member of the Namara Group
27/29 Goodge Street, London W1P 1FD

British Library Cataloguing in Publication Data

Booth, Mark
    Camp.
    1.   Deviant behavior—History
    I.   Title
    302.5'42   HM291

ISBN 0-7043-2353-2

Produced by Cameron Books Limited,
2a Roman Way, London N7 8XG

Edited by Ian Cameron and Jill Hollis
Designed by Ian Cameron
Picture research by Donna Thynne

Printed and bound in Great Britain by
R.J. Acford, Terminus Road Industrial Estate,
Chichester, Sussex

Frontispiece: Danny la Rue and Twiggy in a television spectacular, sequined to the gills, as Jane Russell and Marilyn Monroe singing 'We're just two little girls from Little Rock', the opening number from the film of *Gentlemen Prefer Blondes* (1953).

Title page based on Max Beerbohm's caricature of Aubrey Beardsley.

To Jill Hollis

Contents

Prologue

The audience, numbering about twenty, were seated on a church hall assortment of chairs. Some of them scraped their chairs about on the bare boards to get a better view as the artiste approached the microphone. Eventually the lights dimmed, and a man in a pencil skirt appeared on the stage, to be greeted by a ragged round of applause.

'She' seemed to nod a signal to someone in the wings, and immediately there was a searing crackle from the loudspeakers on either side of the stage—the musical accompaniment, perhaps? But no: a wave of music burst through the crackling bearing its own voice, the pellucid, fragile sound of Diana Ross singing 'Remember Me'. The performer began to mime to it, mouthing the words into the dead microphone, her richly lipsticked lips inching by fits and starts up and down her horse-like teeth. Her eyes remained closed but gently fluttering, as if struggling under the weight of their outrageously large lashes.

Unease seemed to spread through some sections of the audience. There were blazing cheeks and sweaty palms. It was like intruding on something private, watching something that ought not to be watched: safe in the bath, anyone might sing along with the radio or maybe even

mime the words into a mirror, but to have such gaudy and second-rate daydreams acted out in public was excruciating. One felt embarrassed for the performer, and embarrassed for oneself—doubly, because to be seen to be watching this performance, if only by fellow spectators, was like being caught in the act of voyeurism.

'Remember me as a funny day that you once had along the way.' The bony arms that had been pinned to her sides began very slowly and tremulously to move upwards and outwards, so that the lengths of tinsel attached to the underside of her long, silky gloves danced in the footlights; simultaneously her great, pink eyelids began to rise too, the almost tropical luxuriance of her eyelashes opening to reveal great swampy eyes that expressed not sincerity (how could anything be sincere in the context of this travesty?) but possibly a nostalgia for sincerity, the sort you might feel for a very dear and distant moment in childhood. Then, looking again, you saw how overloaded her eyes were, that those gushing glances were being expected to carry more meaning than any glance could; she was not genuinely sentimental, not even genuinely phoney.

'Remember me as a funny clown that made you laugh when you were down.' It was painful to think of this creature as having had a childhood, or indeed any off-stage life. What did he do in the daytime? How did he live? You could imagine him as a mousy little clerk, a

Judy Garland enters the limelight in her last film, *I Could Go On Singing* (1963).

grey flannel suit in the bottom drawer, until the spirit of Diana Ross came and put him on, and raised his predicament to a higher and more glorious plane.

And the strange thing was that against all the odds—the ludicrous nature of the performance, the sordid surroundings—embarrassment was somehow transcended. She flung her arms back in a stylised gesture of abandon. The frenetic swirl of tinselled streamers seemed to gild the air. 'Remember me as a big balloon!' she shrieked, carefully creasing her face with emotion, and a ridiculous new beauty was born, the alien beauty of an insect—gaudy, evanescent material stretched between ugly angular limbs...

There was an explosion of applause from the small audience, part delight and, no doubt, part relief. She blinked and stepped back a pace, the way all artistes do, a limp hand on her chest: 'What me? Surely all this applause can't be for little old me?' Claps, cheers, wolf-whistles. 'Well, I have my little trade, you know. If I can bring a little happiness...' The audience responded with increased applause, which in turn increased the mugging: fighting back the tears, blowing kisses, giggling irrepressibly, there had been nothing like it since Judy Garland in *Babes in Arms!* Yet who, as the applause and the mugging reached a climax, was mocking whom? Were we mocking her by our applause, or was she mocking us by playing up to it? A deep ambivalence suffused her performance—a bashful brashness, a measured spontaneity, a youthfulness older than the rocks. Gloriously glib and titillatingly trite, she claimed a larger significance still: she stood for a proud submissiveness, a depraved chastity that invited adulation whilst repelling admiration, and reduced whatever it touched to absurdity.

This scene, set in a poky club in the back streets of a minor European city, represents something like Christopher Isherwood's view of the quintessence of camp. The club is obscure. It is difficult to find among the strip clubs, the porn shops and the locked-up market stalls. Few go there. Even fewer go a second time. On this view, camp seems very much a minority concern, something very marginal. Yet it is pervasive. If we shift the perspective, we can see camp all around us. Over the last thirty years, writers have seen camp in a great variety of contexts: the parody perversity of 'sixties films such as *Modesty Blaise*, the adult appreciation of children's television programmes such as *Batman*, the tongue-in-cheek revival of former fashion styles, the ironical poking fun at sexual stereotypes in the films of Andy Warhol, even a projected meeting between Mae West and Edith Sitwell.

Campe-toi! Definitions & Origins

Previous views. Fads and fancies. Definition. Confusions: homosexuality, kitsch, theatricality, dandyism, aestheticism, preciosity, pop, chic. Origins and etymology. Monsieur and the Abbé de Choisy. Comedy of Manners. Versailles.

The key to defining camp lies in reconciling its essential marginality with its evident ubiquity, in acknowledging its diversity while still making sense of it.

Recent attempts to define it were sparked off by Christopher Isherwood's discussion of the subject in his novel, *The World in the Evening* (1954). The story concerns the soul-searchings and sexual self-discoveries of a young Englishman in various glamorous locales. One of his self-discoveries is his awakening homosexuality; Isherwood obliquely refers us to the image of a butterfly breaking out of a chrysalis. Tied to this awakening is his realisation of the importance of elegance, or rather, not quite elegance, but camp, which is defined as a matter of 'expressing what's basically serious to you in terms of fun and artifice and elegance' of 'making fun out of' what you take seriously as opposed to making fun of it. Clearly, this is not a definition in the strict sense of the word, its function being suggestive rather than limiting. We may contrive to make our married lives or our office lives fun and/or elegant, but to do this might well be wholesome and even sensible—qualities that are inimical to camp.

His examples may also make us uneasy. To call Mozart camp smacks of impertinence; the Baroque, another candidate, was the militantly optimistic art of the Counter Reformation, designed to overwhelm the spectator with awe for the Catholic Church; it was a mainstream movement of great seriousness even though bits of it may look silly to (some) modern eyes. Perhaps we should pay Isherwood the compliment of believing that when he says that Mozart and the Baroque are camp, he does not mean what he says. What he may mean is that they may be enjoyed (by some people) in a camp way.

The World in the Evening never quite puts its finger on camp. Isherwood is pursued over page after page by the ghost of a good idea, but such is his facility that he manages to evade it.

The next significant examination of the topic, an essay called *Notes on Camp* (1964) by Susan Sontag, suffers from the same kind of confusion. Like Isherwood, Sontag does not hazard a strict definition, but she does go further by positing a series of criteria. Thus camp, according to Sontag, is a way of seeing things as good because they are

11

Above: Marlene Dietrich as naughty, top-hatted Lola in Joseph von Sternberg's *The Blue Angel* (1930).

bad, particularly when: 1) they are marginal, 2) they are artificial or exaggerated, 3) they are *démodé*, 4) they emphasise style at the expense of content, 5) they are objects of the kind prized by daring and witty hedonists, and by 'the Dandies of Mass Culture'.

Sontag is feeling her way around largely unknown territory and, undoubtedly, she bumps up against some interesting points. However, looked at as a whole, the essay presents several difficulties.

It would, perhaps, be churlish to expect anything with a title as modest and down-beat as *Notes on Camp* to be systematic; clearly the vast amount of research Sontag has done on camp has taught her its characteristic technique of forestalling criticisms (*Qui s'accuse, s'excuse*). Nevertheless, she should at least be consistent. Camp is 'unserious', but the rhetoric of General de Gaulle is camp. Wagner and Gide are not camp because they are 'not marginal enough', yet Pope, Congreve, poor old Mozart, Ruskin, Tennyson, Wilde, Burne-Jones and Sarah Bernhardt are all camp. What is 'extravagant in an inconsistent or unpassionate way' is not camp, yet *les précieux* in France, and Wilde, are mentioned as having

Opposite page. Above: Helmut Berger, decadent member of the industrial plutocracy in Nazi Germany, impersonating Dietrich's Lola in Luchino Visconti's *The Damned* (1969). *Below:* a further remove from Lola, though the references are unmistakable. Liza Minnelli brings cheerleader enthusiasm to Bob Fosse's film of the Kander and Ebb musical *Cabaret* (1972) from John van Druten's play *I Am A Camera*, based on Christopher Isherwood's *Goodbye to Berlin*.

been so. 'Who wants to be consistent?' said Wilde 'The dullard and the doctrinaire, the tedious people who carry out their principles to the bitter end of action, the *reductio ad absurdum*. Not I.' Nor Sontag.

The attempt to make sense of *Notes on Camp*, to find its unifying principle, is hindered by its style, and, more particularly, by Sontag's little epigrams, some of which are of an almost oriental inscrutability: 'To name a sensibility, to draw the contours of it, to recount its history, requires a deep sympathy modified by revulsion.'

Her choice of examples needs close attention too. She mentions Des Esseintes in Huysman's *Là-Bas*. Unfortunately Des Esseintes figures in *A Rebours*, not *Là-Bas*. The dandy-like character in Pater's *Marius the Epicurean* is not Marius himself, but Flavius. 'The ideas about morality and politics in *Major Barbara* are camp' she adds impressively. How extraordinary to find Shaw dubbed camp—Shaw, who was a sort of sanitised Nietzsche, a Nietzsche-for-all-the-family.

However, the seriously worrying thing about the examples in *Notes on Camp* is not their intermittent inappropriateness or factual inaccuracy, but their sheer number. A definition of camp that includes Tennyson, the Goon Show, Dali, de Gaulle and children's cartoons is obviously casting the net too wide. In fact, Sontag has difficulty in finding examples of things that, according to her criteria, are not camp; she very properly mentions Jesus, then Napoleon, and Aristophanes's plays (a borderline case perhaps) and Beethoven's quartets (but not apparently the orchestral music?).

The difficulty in this definition is the same as that in Isherwood's; it might be more helpful to say of Tennyson and of children's cartoons not that they are camp, but that they have qualities that invite the patronage of camp people. This would help us to avoid talking as if camp somehow blended into Tennyson or whatever, when camp people began to appreciate them. Camp people and camp objects (that is to say objects made by and for camp people) might then usefully be distinguished from people and objects, which, although not intrinsically camp, appeal to camp people—we might call them camp fads and fancies. This distinction allows a much tighter definition of camp.

Taking examples first from *Notes on Camp*, and then our own, we might illustrate this distinction with two small charts:

A

Camp	Camp fads and fancies
Oscar Wilde, Ronald Firbank	Alfred, Lord Tennyson, Jean Genet
Aubrey Beardsley, some pop art, e.g. Andy Warhol	Edward Burne-Jones, Carlo Crivelli
Mae West, Tallulah Bankhead	Victor Mature, Jane Russell
All About Eve, Beat The Devil	*King Kong, Casablanca, Tom and Jerry*
The Temperance Seven	Wolfgang Amadeus Mozart, *Il Trovatore*

The stylish insolence of Bette Davis in Joseph L. Mankiewicz's *All About Eve* (1950) has found a ready response in the camp. Here she is confronting Anne Baxter, watched by Celeste Holm, George Sanders (as the dandified Addison de Witt), Marilyn Monroe and Hugh Marlowe.

B

Camp	Camp fads and fancies
Dirk Bogarde, Sarah Bernhardt	Judy Garland, Joan Crawford
Interview and *Ritz* magazines	Fanzines
Lindsay Kemp	Nijinsky
P.J. Proby, Soft Cell	Shirley Bassey, Dollar
Fiorucci clothes and accessories	Granny specs, collarless shirts
Solid gold safety pin, real boa constrictor	Real safety pin, feather boa
Rocky Horror Show, Valmouth	*42nd Street, Babes in Arms*
Andy Warhol's *Marilyn*	Kitchener poster: Your Country Needs You
Anglo-catholicism	Catholicism

Even with so few entries, it should immediately be apparent that there is tremendous variety in the right-hand column. The names have very little in common, except that they display qualities likely to endear them to the sort of people in the left-hand column: artificiality, stylisation, theatricality, naivety, sexual ambiguity, tackiness, poor taste, stylishness, the portrayal of camp people (which brings in the novels of Genet). The entries

Left: Judy Garland in *Babes in Arms* (1939). *Below:* Sarah Bernhardt in *L'Aiglon*, Paris, 1900.

Above: Nijinsky in *Giselle*, c1911.
Right: Dirk Bogarde as a Hispanic bad man in a British western, *The Singer Not The Song* (1960).

in the left-hand column, by contrast, are relatively unified. To put it on a wildly fanciful level, you can imagine Wilde, Warhol and Bette Davis getting on famously, but not Tennyson, Genet and Jane Russell. In trying to make sense of both columns together, Isherwood and Sontag were setting themselves an impossible task.

There is one more distinction to be made before we attempt to define camp. It was F.R. Leavis who said of the poets Edith, Osbert and Sacheverell Sitwell that they belonged to the history of publicity rather than of poetry—Oscar Wilde, Andy Warhol and the rest in the 'camp' column have all been successful self-publicists.

Camp is primarily a matter of self-presentation rather than of sensibility. If you are alone and bored at home, and in desperation you try to amuse yourself by watching an awful old film, you are not being camp. You only become so if you subsequently proclaim to others that you thought Victor Mature was divine in *Samson and Delilah*. China ducks on the wall are a serious matter to 'straights', but the individual who displays them in a house of otherwise modernist and modish furniture is being camp.

Building on the work of Isherwood and Sontag, and incorporating the above distinctions, we are now in a position to define camp thus: *To be camp is to present oneself as being committed to the marginal with a commitment greater than the marginal merits.* Everything we should wish to discuss with regard to camp unfolds from this definition.

The primary type of the marginal in society is the traditionally feminine, which camp parodies in an exhibition of stylised effeminacy. In the extent of its commitment, such parody informs the camp person's whole personality, throwing an ironical light not only on the abstract concept of the sexual stereotype, but also on the parodist him or herself. For instance, a non-camp cabaret impressionist may impersonate many film stars, but only so fleetingly and superficially that there is no suggestion that he actually sees himself in terms of these stars. A camp female impersonator, on the other hand, may well continue to use the mannerisms of Bette Davis or Joan Crawford off-stage in a way which says as much about himself as it does about the stars.

Camp self-parody presents the self as being wilfully irresponsible and immature, the artificial nature of the self-presentation making it a sort of off-stage theatricality,

'I am as stylised as it is possible to be' said the poetess Edith Sitwell, here seen in a Cecil Beaton photograph with her two brothers, similarly stylised. Aristocrats themselves, they mocked blue-blooded philistinism and stuffiness, but their flamboyance earned them the suspicion of such less privileged *literati* as F. R. Leavis.

Partridge's cartoon of Oscar Wilde in *Punch*, 1892, accompanied by the caption: 'Quite Too-too puffickly precious. Being Lady Windy-mere's Fan-cy Portrait of the new dramatic author, Shakespeare Sheridan Oscar Puff, Esq.' The verb to puff, in the nineteenth century, meant to advertise with exaggerated praise. No one illustrates better than Oscar Wilde the camp trait of excessive self-advertisement. *The Daily Telegraph* reported that he 'addressed from the stage a public audience, mostly composed of ladies, pressing between his daintily-gloved fingers a still burning and half-smoked cigarette.'

the shameless insincerity of which may be provocative, but also forestalls criticism by its ambivalence. Non-camp people are occasionally frivolous as a holiday from moral seriousness; camp people are only occasionally not frivolous.

Other types of the marginal are the trivial, the trashy, the kitsch and the not-terribly-good. Thus, in the cultural sphere, to be camp is to be perversely committed to the trash aesthetic or to a sort of 'cultural slumming', (a phrase of Richard Hoggart's in *The Uses of Literacy*), which, being in theory incomprehensible to non-camp people, becomes fashionably exclusive.

Camp art is art that sympathetically, stylishly and attractively represents camp behaviour, or represents a non-camp subject in a camp way. In the case of decorative art, camp objects are those made by camp people to decorate the camp life-style. A work of art may be verified as camp if we catch in it a reflection of a camp ambiguity in the mind of its creator.

This neater, tidier definition maintains the distinction between camp and camp's fads and fancies, and it also helps to distinguish camp from various related phenomena with which it is often confused. It is worth taking a look at some of these confusions.

Troglodytes sometimes confuse camp with homosexual. The unhelpful idea that camp originated in homosexual cliques in the 'thirties was aired by Isherwood, popularised by Sontag, and has remained unquestioned in subsequent discussion. However, as we shall see, camp's origins are far from being so humble. Undoubtedly, the effeminate strain in leading camp personalities such as Beau Brummell and Andy Warhol has caused many to think of them as homosexuals, but, although some may have been squeamish about women, this hardly constitutes homosexual behaviour. Camp people tend to be asexual rather than homosexual. Brummell *et al* were perhaps honorary homosexuals, or homosexuals in spirit rather than in practice. In camp culture, the popular image of the homosexual, like the popular image of the feminine woman, is mimicked as a type of the marginal. So, while it may be true that many homosexuals are camp, only a small proportion of people who exhibit symptoms of camp behaviour are homosexual.

Another common confusion is between camp and kitsch, which, as Roland Barthes has written, 'implies a recognition of high aesthetic values': it represents an

While camp may toy with bad taste, kitsch embraces it: the monument to Luigi Berlando (1952) in Staglieno cemetery in Genoa, Léon Frédéric's pink and blue painting *Le Torrent*, and a Berlin production of *Madame Butterfly*, c1906.

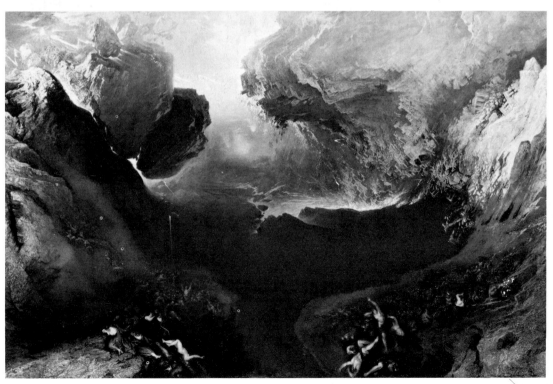

unwitting failure on a massive scale. French Symbolist paintings are kitsch, and so are the apocalyptic fantasies of John Martin; the marble stadium that Mussolini built outside Rome is kitsch, as is his railway station in Milan, where even the concrete cherubs have the bald head and bull-neck of *il Duce*; the American Declaration of Independence is kitsch, as are most Sword-and-Sorcery science fiction and most Heavy Rock music; many people find Wagner's operas kitsch. 'The worst art is always done with the best intentions,' said Oscar Wilde, perhaps providing the key to the distinction between kitsch and camp. Unlike kitsch, camp does not even have honourable intentions. Yet, although kitsch is never intrinsically camp, it has a certain toe-curling quality that appeals to the camp sense of humour. Kitsch is one of camp's favourite fads and fancies.

Off-stage theatricality, though not synonymous with camp, is certainly a common manifestation of it: camp people use the exaggerated gestures of the theatre to draw

Edith Sitwell as a Gothic tomb carving, photographed by Cecil Beaton, 1927.

Opposite page. Top: National Socialist kitsch—Hitler Youth at the Nuremberg Rally in Leni Riefenstahl's *Triumph of the Will* (1936). *Bottom:* John Martin's *The Great Day of His Wrath* (1851-53).

attention to themselves, a technique epitomised by Sarah Bernhardt. In her day, she was seen as taking off-stage theatricality as far as it would go. Nicknamed Sarah Barnum because of her tireless publicity-seeking, she drew attention to herself by wearing drag, sleeping in a quilted coffin and surrounding herself with exotic pets—a cheetah, six chameleons, a parrot called Bizibouzon and a monkey called Darwin. Her public persona was so outlandish that it seemed to vindicate even the most bizarre rumour. At one time, she was said to play croquet with skulls that she had dressed up in Louis XIV wigs. On stage, theatricality can be camp when the play itself is camp (e.g. *The Importance of Being Earnest*), when camp person is being portrayed (e.g. *The Staircase*) or when actors send a play up by deliberately over-acting.

The phenomenon that best accomodates itself to comparison with camp is dandyism. At this point, the Victorian moralist, Thomas Carlyle should make his entrance, with his portly little figures of speech trotting after him, for he it was, in *Sartor Resartus* (1834),who set about defining dandyism. 'A Dandy is a Clothes-wearing Man' he wrote, 'a Man whose trade, office and existence consists in the wearing of Clothes. Every faculty of his soul, spirit, purse and person is heroically consecrated to this one object, the wearing of clothes wisely and well: so that as others dress to live, he lives to dress.'

Above: Sarah Bernhardt in *Leah*. She would surely have agreed with Jean Cocteau's aphorism: '*Un peu trop, pour moi c'est assez*'. *Left:* scene from the original private production of John Osborne's *A Patriot for Me*.

Carlyle then goes on to highlight the hollowness of dandyism (as he understands it) by suggesting in a *recherché* simile that it bears 'a not inconsiderable resemblance to that superstition of the Athos Monks who, by fasting from all nourishment and looking intensely for a length of time into their own navels, came to discern therein the true Apocalypse of Nature and Heaven Unveiled.'

Carlyle's jokes will always be greeted with the reverence they deserve. Fervidly anti-dandy, he was concerned to discredit them, and duly did. But a closer examination reveals various aspects of the dandy that refuse to submit to Carlyle's authority. For instance, to see the original dandy, Beau Brummell, as simply a 'Clothes-wearing Man' is to diminish him to such an extent that he ceases to be recognisable. When Brummell's friend Byron said that there were three great men in the nineteenth century, Brummell, Napoleon and himself, he was evidently not anticipating Carlyle's view of Brummell merely as the man who invented trousers.

In his own lifetime, Brummell's reputation was principally as a wit. He is supposed to have said of the Prince Regent (later George IV), 'I made him what he is, and I can unmake him.' He also uttered the maxim: 'A well-tied tie is a man's first serious step in life.' and 'I like

Humming Birds or A Dandy Trio, 1818, by George Cruikshank.

to have the morning well-aired before I get up.' In fact, Brummell was the originator of that exclusive wit and provocative frivolity which we tend to think of today as inimitably Wildean, but which was really (all-too-imitably) Brummellian. He was also a collector of snuff-boxes, china plate and *bibelots*, and he wrote Society verses including the famous *Butterfly Funeral*.

Brummell's spirit (and, after Brummell's, the dandy's) was consecrated not, as Carlyle supposed, simply to clothes, but to trivia, of which clothing was one example, along with pretty witticisms, snuff-boxes, verse and all the rest. Carlyle mistook an instance for the principle.

Nowhere does dandyism's campness come across better than in the Silver Fork novels; it was these novels of dialogue and decor that Oscar Wilde was avowedly trying to revive with *The Picture of Dorian Gray*. Written by followers of the Beau, and usually containing fictionalised portraits of him, they purported to depict the *beau monde* accurately. The first Silver Fork novel, written in 1825, was Plumer Ward's *Tremaine*, and Benjamin Disraeli wrote *Vivian Grey* in 1826. The two outstanding examples, however, were Thomas Lister's *Granby* (1826) and George Bulwer-Lytton's *Pelham: the Adventures of a Gentleman* (1828).

Granby contains an extended portrait of Brummell in the guise of Trebeck, 'the most powerful poseur of his year'. We follow him in his intrigues through the world of Dandy clubs, balls, the ballet and the opera. The tone is best conveyed by snatches of dialogue:

'I solemnly assure you,' said Trebeck, that nothing was further from my intention than a compliment. Compliments are mauvais ton—are they not Lady Elizabeth? They are quite obsolete—went out with hoops and hair powder. Pray do not accuse me of wishing to revive them.'

'...Lord Chesterton—a man deeply impressed with his own consequence, but not at all skilled in the art of impressing others with it.'

The eponymous dandy hero of *Pelham* moves in similarly flippant circles. The book begins:

'The end of the season was unusually dull, and my mother, having looked over her list of engagements, and ascertained that she had none worth staying for, agreed to elope with her new lover.'

Confusion between camp and aestheticism perhaps arose out of Oscar Wilde's early aesthetic pose. In fact, Wilde was never a true aesthete. Aesthetes want to see; camp people such as Wilde, prefer to be seen. Where the aesthete makes his life a work of art, the camp person tries to do the same with his personality. The sociable some-sometimes socialite literature of camp should not be confused with the sad, solitary pleasures of the aesthete and his grubby cultivation of his mental garden. Camp literature is easily accessible and light-hearted; aesthetic literature is troubled by a Poe-faced symbolism. Serious aesthetes tend to be priggish, whilst camp people gaily publicise themselves as immoral.

Wilde's aestheticism was primarily a means of shocking others. He was relatively uninterested in nurturing inner-directed experiences, but espoused a sort of comic aestheticism. In his essay *Pen, Pencil and Poison*, he relates with obvious approval the story of the flamboyant

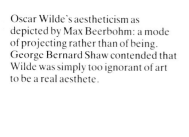

Oscar Wilde's aestheticism as depicted by Max Beerbohm: a mode of projecting rather than of being. George Bernard Shaw contended that Wilde was simply too ignorant of art to be a real aesthete.

dandy Thomas Griffiths Wainewright, who murdered a girl called Helen Abercrombie, and, when reproached by a friend, shrugged his shoulders and said, 'Yes, it was a dreadful thing to do, but she had very thick ankles.' Wainewright's quip was evidently a springboard for much of Wilde's humour.

The illustrators and printers Charles Ricketts *(right)* and C.H. Shannon *(left)*, who collaborated with Wilde on some of his early aesthetic books. Their home in Chelsea was said by Wilde to be 'the one house in London where a visitor is never bored'; he called them Orchid and Marigold.

Another confusing term is preciosity, or indeed, *préciosité*. Our understanding of the *précieux* has been much coloured by Molière's comedy *Les Précieuses Ridicules*, which guys the pretensions to *préciosité* of two young country girls:

'Come and hold for us the counsellor of the graces,' says one of the girls to a servant.

'Gracious me!' replies the servant, 'I don't know what creature that is: you must talk like a Christian if you want me to understand you.'

'Bring us the looking-glass, you ignoramus, and take care not to contaminate its surface with the reflection of your image.'

Understanding *préciosité* in terms of a comedy, we are perhaps apt to forget that it was partly a serious-minded movement concerned to refine and to clarify the French language. Some of its more extreme refinements and 'clarifications' may now seem silly and affected, but we should be wary of calling them camp on that account.

French critics make a useful distinction between mainstream *préciosité* and *coquetterie*, the latter being the fun-loving and irreverent aspect of *préciosité* that required poets to exercise their ingenuity in writing elegant banter to amuse salon guests—for example, verses to accompany the gift of a bouquet of flowers or to commemorate the death of a parrot. This sort of good-humoured commitment to the marginal might justifiably be called camp.

To be precious, then, is not the same as to be camp—humourless preciousness is not camp—but there is a vein of camp behaviour that is precious and is characterised by a humorous fastidiousness and mock-feminine hypochondria. A camp character in Ronald Firbank's *The Flower beneath the Foot*, complains that he has 'a hundred headaches.'

In *Revolt into Style* (1970), George Melly pointed out that in the 'sixties, pop was more or less synonymous with camp. And if we look at Richard Hamilton's famous list of the attributes of pop, we can draw up a very similar list of attributes of camp, at least the camp of television entertainment and media advertising.

Pop		*Camp*	
	Popular (designed for mass audiences)		Easily accessible
	Transient (short-term solutions)		Determinedly facile
	Expendable		Trashy
	Low cost		Mock luxurious
	Mass-produced		Mass-produced
	Young		Youth worshipping
	Witty		Witty
	Sexy		Mock sexy
	Gimmicky		Wilfully hackneyed
	Glamorous		Mock glamorous
	Big business		BIG BUSINESS

Some twenty years later, it is much easier to avoid confusing pop with camp. Although camp has been an important factor in determining the style of pop, it has become mixed with other styles—negro, folk, country, music hall and Hollywood razzmatazz. And although pop has served to jazz up and help popularise camp, it did no more than that, for camp is a much older (by some three hundred years) and bigger phenomenon, taking in aspects of High Culture as well as popular performance.

Nowadays, if camp is liable to be confused with any one word, it is not with pop but with chic. Lucinda and Piers may seem very camp as they trip lightly from the social columns of *Vogue* to *The Tatler* and back again, but one need only remind oneself of the 'fifties when doughty debs, charms all too palpable, were herded up from the country to be decked out in ropes of pearls and chiffons, to realise that this connection between camp and chic is, like the one between camp and pop, a matter of historical accident rather than conceptual necessity. Chic is, of course, the quality which the French regard themselves as having to a superlative degree, but it carries with it no implication that they regard themselves as being in any way marginal; on the contrary, they take it more as a mark of their racial superiority. Similarly, Shirley Temple may be very chic as an American ambassador, but she does not intend thereby to be camp. True chic is an expression through extreme elegance of superior power, as opposed to camp which is a self-mocking abdication of any pretensions to power.

An examination of the origins and etymology of camp provides historical support for my definition.

The far-fetched, the bogus and the patently ludicrous will always cluster round camp. There have been many extraordinary explanations of its origin. As Philip Howard recorded in *Old Words for New*, it has been located in the police files of New York City as KAMP (Known As Male Prostitute), as the name of homosexual brothels in the Australian outback of the nineteenth century, and as a slang word used by dandies to describe their assignations with soldiers spending the summer under canvas in London's Hyde Park. Colourful as these etymologies are, they must regrettably be discarded as retrojections of today's Isherwoodian and Sontagesque misconceptions.

Sontag asserts that before her essay, camp had only broken into print in Isherwood's *The World in the Evening* (published in 1954, not as she claims in 1948). But the word appears in at least one essay by the popular American journalist, Tom Wolfe, *The Girl of the Year* (published 1963); and in the same year, the English literary mandarin Cyril Connolly wrote a spoof on spy fiction called *Bond Strikes Camp* (in which the beautiful Russian spy turns out to be 'M' in drag.) Sontag could also have mentioned Angus Wilson's 1952 novel, *Hemlock and After* which refers, among other usages, to 'the blond malice of Sherman's camp chatter'. Even earlier Constant Lambert wrote in *Music Ho! A Study of Music in Decline* (1934): 'The change in style observable between the pre-war and post-war Diaghilev ballets reflects the purely fashionable change in the tastes of the concentration camp of intellectuals to whom Diaghilev played up.' And, 'With the minor Parisian figures, the camp followers of Diaghilev, it is fairly safe to assume that lack of individuality and desire for chic were at the back of their changes of style.' That the word 'camp' is used twice in the context of the camp people who gathered around Diaghilev is surely not a coincidence.

Ware's dictionary of *Passing English of the Victorian Era*, published in 1909, says this of camp: 'actions and gestures of an exaggerated emphasis. Probably from the French. Used chiefly of persons of exceptional want of character, e.g., "How very camp he is."

Coco Chanel photographed by Cecil Beaton, 1937.

Above: Flamingo-footed Robert de Montesquiou-Fezensac, perhaps the most extravagantly camp character of the *Belle Epoque*, dressed as Louis XIV.

Opposite: '*Matamore se campait*'—an illustration by Gustave Doré for the 1865 edition of Théophile Gautier's novel *Le Capitaine Fracasse*.

Following Ware, we find *se camper* in Théophile Gautier's *Capitaine Fracasse* (1863)—an elaborate and witty spoof on the Romantic novel, written in a lush, decadent style that he created as a pastiche of *préciosité*. It concerns an impoverished young baron who sets out to make his fortune, joining up with a wandering troupe of actors on their way to Paris. Matamore, a stock character among the comedians of the troupe, makes a fool of himself by falling in love with a lady, Isabelle, whose affections lie elsewhere. This vainglorious poseur defiantly presents the gift of his body to Isabelle: '*Matamore se campait dans une pose extravagemment anguleuse dont sa maigreur excessive faisait encore ressortir le ridicule.*' [Matamore camped it up in an extravagantly angular pose which his great thinness served to make even more ridiculous.]

Gautier is apparently using *se camper* here with the associations of an army camp. *Se camper* is to present oneself in an expansive but flimsy manner (like a tent), with overtones here of theatricality, vanity, dressiness, and provocation.

Tracing the origin of this sense of *se camper* provides a valuable signpost to the origin of the whole phenomenon. It is interesting that *Capitaine Fracasse* is set in the seventeenth century, of which it presents a nostalgic portrait, for camp people have always idealised seventeenth-century France, above all because of Louis XIV and Versailles.

Prinnie, the Prince Regent, and 'mad' Ludwig II of Bavaria justified their camp architectural follies by reference to Louis XIV: Versailles was the place where Robert de Montesquiou-Fezensac (who was the model for Marcel Proust's Baron de Charlus) held some of his legendary parties. In the novel *Venus and Tannhäuser*, Venusberg is Aubrey Beardsley's pornographic vision of Versailles, while the fearsome eyes of Vathek in William Beckford's Gothick novel, capable of knocking people backwards with just a glance, are the fabled eyes of Louis XIV.

Camp people look back on Louis XIV's Versailles as a sort of camp Eden, a self-enclosed world devoted to *divertissements*, to dressing-up, showing off, and scandal —in fact the world captured in Madame de la Fayette's *La Princesse de Clèves* (1678). 'There is only one thing worse than going to a party with one's beloved,' she wrote, 'and that is not going with her.' How evocative that proto-Wildean sentiment is of a camp ambiance! The world Madame de la Fayette describes is one of an indefinitely prolonged adolescence, an interplay of appearance, pretence and deceit in the midst of which the greatest joy was 'to note the effect of one's beauty on others', where the greatest worry was keeping up with the latest fashion, and where love was always mixed with cynicism, and cynicism with love: auspicious circumstances for the ascendancy of camp.

Louis XIV's well-known policy of diverting the nobility from politics by means of fêtes and other such Versailles entertainments (Walpole called Versailles 'a toy' and 'a garden for a great child')—in effect, the policy of manoeuvring the nobles into the margins of French life, made Versailles a paradigm of high camp society.

All camp people are to be found in the margins of society, and the richest vein of camp is generally to be found in the margins of the margins. Marginal to the king's own set at Versailles was that of his brother, 'the king of mischief makers', known simply as 'Monsieur'. Modelling his personal style on that of the effeminate Henri III, Monsieur surrounded himself with exquisites. He had been educated to be totally ignorant of all political and practical matters (so as not to be a threat to the king), possibly spending part of his childhood in girls' clothes: he

Three effeminate minions of the court of Henri III illustrate the style of adornment favoured by Philippe, Duc d'Orléans. *Three Princes*, School of Fontainebleau, 1580s.

Philippe, Duc d'Orléans, Louis XIV's disreputable brother, who was known as 'Monsieur'.

grew up to wear rings, bracelets, ribbons, women's jewellery, perfume and sometimes even rouge. He was notorious for his underworld connections, for his irreverence (it was believed he used to take a large missal every day to mass, until someone found he was reading Rabelais), for his sodomy and for many things much too disgusting to include here. Monsieur's fêtes, without the ballast of power-affirming symbolism that the king's presence imposed, floated off into camp fantasy. He liked to throw parties to which everyone went as shepherds and shepherdesses—a pastime which, because of her peasant village at the Petit Trianon, we tend to associate more with Marie-Antoinette. Anne-Marie d'Orléans describes how she and Monsieur (who had by now totally abandoned himself to absurdity with his minute cherry

Le Petit Hameau by Joseph Carand, showing the miniature farm playground where Marie Antoinette amused herself with friends in peasant costume.

mouth and the record of his gluttony stretching out in front of him) dressed in silver fabric bordered with red piping and wore aprons of black velvet covered with red, white and black plumes, with their hair dressed in the style of the peasants of Bresse; they also carried shepherds' crooks of red lacquer decorated with silver. 'Bodily toil frees us from mental trouble,' said the *précieux* philosopher, the Duc de la Rochefoucauld, 'and that is what makes the poor so happy.'

There is another first hand account of Monsieur's set in a passage in the bizarre *Transvestite Memoirs of the Abbé de Choisy*, who was a well-known chronicler of court and church affairs. These memoirs provide a fascinating record of his and Monsieur's secret eccentricities.

'I opened five or six buttonholes at the bottom of my gown, in order to reveal a robe of speckled black satin, the train of which was not as long as the gown. I also wore a white damask underskirt, which could be seen only when the train was carried. I ceased to wear trunk hose; to me it was hardly becoming to a woman, and I had no fear of being cold because it was full summer. I had a muslin cravat, whose tassels dropped on a huge knot of

Les Plaisirs de la Campagne, illustration from *La Gazette du Bon Ton* for a summer dress by Poiret, 1921.

black ribbon which was attached to the top of my *robe de chambre*. The gown revealed my shoulders which always remained quite white through the great care I had taken of them all my life; every morning, I lathered my neck with veal water and sheep's foot grease, which made the skin soft and white.'

He tries to come to terms with his tastes:

'The attribute of God is to be loved, adored. Man, as far as the weakness of his nature allows, wishes for the same, but, as it is beauty that kindles love and since that is usually the lot of women, when it happens that men have, or believe themselves to have, certain traits of beauty, they try to enhance them by the same methods that women use, which are most becoming. They feel the inexpressible pleasure of being loved. I have felt this more than once during a delightful affair. When I was at a ball or the theatre, wearing my beautiful *robe de chambre*, diamonds and patches, and heard people murmur near me, "There is a lovely woman", I experienced an inward glow of pleasure which is incomparable, it is so strong. Ambition, riches, even love do not equal it, because we always love ourselves more deeply than we do others.'

Louis XIV dressed in a fanciful interpretation of Roman costume.

But his happiest hours were spent in the company of Monsieur—'I went to the Palais-Royal whenever Monsieur was in Paris. He was almost effusively friendly to me, because we had the same inclinations. He longed to dress as a woman himself, but did not dare, because of his position (princes are prisoners of their rank). In the evenings he would put on cornets, ear pendants and patches, and gaze at his reflection in a mirror.

'Fulsomely flattered by his admirers, he gave a great ball every year on Shrove Monday. He ordered me to attend in a loose robe, my face unmasked and instructed the Chevalier de Fradine to lead me in the *courante*.

'It was a splendid assembly; there were at least 34 women decked with pearls and diamonds. I was admired, I danced to perfection, and it seemed the ball was made for me.

'Monsieur opened it with Mademoiselle de Brancas, who was very pretty (she later became the Princesse d'Harcourt) and a moment later he went to dress up as a woman and returned to the ball masked. Everyone recognised him, just as he intended, and the Chevalier de Lorraine tendered him his hand. He danced the minuet and then went to sit amongst all the ladies. He had to be persuaded a little before he would remove his mask, although secretly this was all he wished to do, as he longed to be seen by everyone. It is impossible to describe the extent of his coquetry in admiring himself, putting on patches and then changing their positions. But perhaps I would have been worse. Men, once they think they are beautiful, are far more besotted with their appearance than women are.'

In view of all this camping at Versailles, it is appropriate that what may have been the earliest mention of *se camper* in our sense is to be found in *Les Fourberies de Scapin*, a play by Louis XIV's beneficiary, Molière, first performed in 1671. It appears in a passage that Gautier may, consciously or unconsciously, have been echoing—a suggestion reinforced by the fact that Matamore's valet in *Capitaine Fracasse* is called Scapin.

In *Les Fourberies de Scapin*, the rascally valet Scapin persuades Octavio to bluff his way out of trouble with his father by dressing up as a stage villain and prancing around in front of him in a provocative manner:

'Wait, stop a minute,' says Scapin to Octavio, as the idea dawns on him, and he begins to see the possibilities, 'Stick your hat on at an angle and look disreputable. Camp about on one leg ('*campe-toi sur un pied*'). Put your hand on your hip. Strut like a comedy-king!'

To understand the peculiar connotations of *se camper*, it is helpful to know a bit about army camps in France at this time. The idea of tents did not then call to mind the small

The transvestite Abbé de Choisy holding his clerical robe up in a feminine manner.

s. leClerc f.

Camp life: sketch by Jacques Callot of an army officer.

Below: Louis MacNeice at Cambridge in the 1930s.

khaki, utilitarian apologies of today, but great billowy creations of shining fabrics—satins and silks studded with jewels, tapestries and gold banners.

When Louis XIV went on manoeuvres, the courtiers who had been camping out in the apartments, rooms and corridors of Versailles, de-camped to follow the king. If they did not fight, they at least moved to a respectful distance from the fighting, to watch. In fact, as Saint-Simon recorded, the spectacle and the display of court life was transferred to camp, which differed only in its lightness and its impermanence. The camp was an insubstantial pageant, a byword for transient magnificence where men were encouraged to wear their finest costumes, to preen themselves—indeed, to advertise themselves.

Camp behaviour was not thought incompatible with good soldiering—if anything, the reverse. Monsieur himself loved battles, not only for the exercise (part of the ever-futile fight to keep himself trim) but also because of the opportunity for swanking. The De Villiers Journal recounts a young French officer's complaints about camp life's drain on his purse: the expensive items were not, it seems, irrelevancies like weapons, but clothes, carriages and silver plate.

Again, the element of off-stage theatricality in Molière's use of *se camper* is significant. Puritans, both religious and secular, have always worried about the effect of theatre on moral seriousness; theatre falsifies the self, encourages insincerity and promotes frivolity.

40

Versailles in its more camp aspects might have embodied their worst fears. Anthony Blunt (an account of whose own very camp schooldays is to be found in Louis MacNeice's autobiography) has noted that in the courts of this time the borderlines between stage and off-stage, between fête and daily life, were very vague. Often a masque or a play such as *Le Bourgeois Gentilhomme* would culminate in a ball, an invitation to which was extended to the whole audience.

In 1661, Mademoiselle de Sévigné recorded in her letters how the king would sometimes appear in costume on stage—sometimes even in ballets—and how, at other times, when carnivals spread through the streets surrounding the palace, he would mask himself and slip off into the crowd incognito, to who knows what assignations. Some people detected an air of pasteboard about the whole institution of the monarchy; the Prince de Conti referred to Louis XIV in a letter as '*le Roi de théâtre*' and was banished—the barb seems to have hit home. Amorality succeeded morality, and stylishness replaced graciousness: the courtiers in the pictures of contemporary artists such as Callot are consummate stylists, behaving almost as if they are on-stage, walking with a swaggering, dance-like action which in their day (if Molière's usage was not unique) would have been called *se campant*, and which we should call 'camping it up'. If we translate their hyperbolic gestures into twentieth century terms, we see queens lolloping about underneath the streetlights of Berlin or Mae West shakin' the shimmy.

Of course, Louis XIV did not build Versailles with the intention of making it camp, but, like peasants after a revolution, camp people have camped out in the palace. They have overrun the legend of Versailles and converted it to camp. Versailles stands in camp memory, not, as it was intended, as a symbol of Decorative Absolutism, but as a symbol of Absolute Decorativism.

Above: Le roi du théâtre. Louis XIV dressed as the Sun King at a masquerade. *Right:* sketch by Jacques Callot of a seventeenth-century French nobleman *se campant.*

Camping Sites

Sources: city life, pluralism, style, learning. Targets: conventional morality, good taste, marriage and family, suburbia, sport, business. Pastimes: boredom, divertisse-ments, scandal, self-decoration, exclusivism. Divine decadence. Conformity.

Little in history is objectively verifiable as camp. Camp is so much a matter of a raised eyebrow, a secret smile, an almost imperceptible pout or the barest suggestion of a limp wrist (the little signs that push the persona into parody) that, except in the few cases where the word camp or *se camper* have been used, it is difficult to pin down.

In his diary entry for 1st July 1663, Samuel Pepys records:

'After dinner we fell in talking. Mr Batten telling us of a late trial of Sir Charles Sedley the other day for his debauchery a little while since at Oxford Gates; coming in open day into the Balcone and showed his nakedness—acting all the postures of lust and buggery that could be imagined and abusing of scripture…a thousand people standing underneath to see and hear him.'

The comedies of the time suggest that camp behaviour was then rife, and Pepys's account includes qualities that are often a mark of it—exhibitionism, humour, posturing and intimations of sexual deviation. And yet we cannot be sure that what is being described is camp. Sedley's antics might, for all we can tell from the description, have been the boisterous crudity which we associate today with hearties on the razzle, or they might have been expressions of the reckless nihilism more usually associated with Sedley's contemporary Rochester; in neither case would Sedley's behaviour have been camp.

Camp, as we have seen, is a matter of parody; as such, it borrows much of its form from the object of its parody. Chameleon-like, the camp person takes on the colours of the society that supports him—except that they are not quite the same colours, being tinged with a particular irony. In a society that is silly, lewd and affected, you find the camp person: mock silly, mock lewd and mock affected. Camp is not frivolity itself but a certain malformation of frivolity. Too often, the tools of historical analysis are not sharp enough to make these distinctions and that which was simply silly becomes mock silly in retrospect.

There is little point, then, in attempting a chronological history of camp. On the other hand, even with sparse evidence, a picture can be drawn of the social structures

The camp require an urban environment in order to indulge their taste for parading themselves. Photograph by David Bailey.

that are conducive to camp. We can look back, even beyond Versailles, to see the first stirrings of camp, and we can trace the origins of some of its deeper impulses. Even with only circumstantial evidence, and even where camp itself has perished, it is perhaps possible to piece together a camp-shaped mould.

When the subject of camp is under discussion, certain places and times irresistibly suggest themselves: Versailles, Regency England, the Belle Epoque. These are history's camping sites, and it is in their literature, their memoirs and their art that we can occasionally catch the genuine flavour of camp. Fitting together these disparate items of ephemera, which are our only direct evidence, we may begin to fill out our camp-shaped mould.

First, basics. Camp is a product of urban life: it seems that the bigger the urban complex, the more likely it is to produce camp. 'Anything worth doing is worth doing in public,' said Joe Orton. The camp person must have a

AUTHOR OF "VIVIAN GREY."

Benjamin Disraeli.
The young Disraeli adopted the dandyism of Brummell to which he added a lush and colourful flamboyance of his own. John Bright said of him, 'He is a self-made man who worships his creator.'

public to perform to: he needs simply to be near large numbers of people. The stare of the crowd is the sun towards which camp bends. Camp people luxuriate in the different shades of admiration. They harvest the glances of others with an efficiency that would be heroic, were the concept of heroism not inimical to camp. There is something of the *boulevardier*, of the *flâneur* about some camp people. In his diary, the young Disraeli (the 'Jew d'esprit') records uninhibited delight that his costume—a blue *surtout*, a pair of light blue trousers and black stockings with red stripes—caused a sensation in Regent Street. 'The people,' he wrote, 'quite made way for me as I passed! It was like the parting of the Red Sea, which I now perfectly believe from experience.' To a certain temperament, the very anonymity of city life invites such exhibitionism. It is a challenge. Having risked public contempt, Disraeli won public admiration.

City life also appeals to camp in its flashy, worldly and pleasure-seeking side, in its superficiality and its immediacy. The demands it makes upon alertness and spontaneity, verbal facility and putting up a front find a ready response in camp people. In fact, camp is attracted by the sheer unnaturalness of the city.

Camp people have always shown markedly unfilial feelings towards Mother Nature. A bore back from a holiday in the Lake District asked Brummell which lake he preferred. Brummell turned to his valet:

'Robinson' he said, 'which of the lakes *do* I admire?'

'Windermere, sir.'

'Ah yes—Windermere,' he replied, 'so it is—Windermere.'

And in answer to an earnest American girl's question, Brian Howard remarked: 'Yes, I dare say the forests of New England are very nice in the Fall, but I fear they would be too garish for me.'

'Nature,' said Oscar Wilde, reaching for the most damning epithet to hand, 'is middle-class.'

The idea of the city as a breeding ground for camp leads back to the sixteenth century which, it is commonly accepted, saw the beginning of a significant breakdown of the agriculture-based social hierarchy. Society went into a state of flux and fragmentation that had important implications for the creation of camp. The increasingly complex nature of city life, in particular, had an unsettling effect. It meant that, for the first time, a man might be able to choose his rôle in life. Not only that, but in the course of several days, he might be forced to adapt his personality to the values of the different social groups he might meet, experiencing for the first time one facet of the phenomenon that sociologists call pluralism. 'Knowing people's different dispositions, a man must alter his style according to that of the person with whom he is conversing,' said Baldassare Castiglione. That such a thing was considered worth saying then (today we take it for granted) suggests that it was a relatively new phenomenon.

This experience of the relativity of social roles encouraged man to stand outside his personality and to see it as something of a put-on, something artificial. City life came to be understood as actually *requiring* people to lead large parts of their lives insincerely. Instead of having a personality integral to himself, a man availed himself of a series of off-the-peg personalities. The more choices of personality he had, the more detached he seemed to feel from all of them and the more difficult he found it to take any one of them seriously. It is but a short step from this experience of alienation to the exploration of its ironic possibilities that lies at the heart of camp.

'Most people are other people,' complained the young Wilde. 'Their thoughts are someone else's opinions, their lives a mimicry, their passions a quotation.' Later, he would crow, 'What most people call insincerity is simply a method by which we multiply our personalities.'

'I, too,' said Max Beerbohm with sardonic glee, 'have my Elizabethan moments, my Caroline moments. I have gone to bed Georgian and awoken Early Victorian.'

We are accustomed to talk as if a preoccupation with personal style were something new. In fact, it was another product of the sixteenth century. As manners ceased to be an expression of a rigidly hierarchical society, and became instead more flexible, they increasingly admitted of changes and ultimately fashions. As communications improved, society became more cosmopolitan and a greater variety of styles became available. The more sophisticated courts, detaching themselves from harsh political and economic necessities, became lighter, brighter and more frivolous. It was their policy, in anticipation of Versailles, to keep courtiers occupied with mere mischief in an endless round of entertainments. Manners became more leisure-orientated.

The erosion of the values of birth and inherited wealth also promoted the importance of self-conscious self-presentation as a means of acquiring wealth or achieving office. Appearances came to the fore: success could be a matter of personal style—an eventuality without which camp would have been inconceivable.

The word *maniera* was used to describe the qualities of a courtier in these circumstances—effortlessly superior, elegant, poised and polished. The ideal was to cut a dash. Life became more artificial and less sincere. Out of this atmosphere grew Castiglione's *The Courtier* (published in 1528), which spread the lifestyle throughout Europe. Cardinal Mazarin caused a new influx of things Italian into the France of Louis XIII, and the adoption of Italian manners—sumptuous spectacles, masked balls, worldly morals and a quick and ironical wit.

'In Venice,' says the Countess in Firbank's *The Flower Beneath the Foot*, 'the indecent movement of the gondoliers quite affected my health.' Carpaccio's idealised depictions of an artificial and sophisticated Venice peopled by elegant young men have always appealed to the camp. Detail from *A Miracle of the Relic of the True Cross*.

47

But as fast as manners came to ripeness in the courts, they came to overripeness and affectation around the margins. Castiglione's ideal courtier and the honnête homme in France and England were urged to moderation: 'Beyond certain bounds, the man of taste ends and the frivolous virtuoso begins'—among such virtuosi, camp is liable to arise. 'Affectations in moderation are merely tedious, but when exaggerated they can be very funny,' wrote Castiglione; such a thought might well offer a starting point for camp.

In the artistic sphere, the developments in manners were reflected in Mannerism—a movement squeezed in between High Renaissance and Baroque. In Mannerism, there is a facility, a panache and a capriciousness that is the analogue in paint of the flourishes and epigrams of the courtier. As John Shearman has noted, techniques that originally had an emotive purpose were exploited for purely aesthetic effect. Aesthetics can only be elevated in this way at the expense of ethics. Religious motifs received the same treatment. The Madonnas painted by the Mannerist Parmigianino, for example, would not look out of place modelling leather underwear. Inventive and stagey, frisky and cerebral, Mannerist paintings were produced with fashionable, pleasure-seeking audiences in mind. And where culture is sophisticated in this way, there is always a possibility that it will shade off into camp.

Rosso and Primaticcio, two of Parmigianino's close contemporaries, were engaged in the 1530s to decorate the French royal palace at Fontainebleau. What remains of their work—principally the paintings framed by stuccos in the Galérie François I—shows some sign of Parmigianino's influence. The paintings are brightly-coloured depictions of elongated, elegant, almost sybaritic figures acting out religious or, more usually, mythological stories. Inevitably, indigenous French painters copied the Italian style. Among them, the courtly Antoine Caron is perhaps of special interest because of his sociable, modish version of Mannerism which reflected the frivolous atmosphere of the court fêtes that he helped to organise. Caron's revellers embody a camp ideal of bodily beauty. Their hands are too small, too nervous for serious work, and their heads too small for serious thought—the apotheosis of the pin-head; then, as now, the idle rich regarded intelligence as infra dig.

It is tempting to claim much of Mannerism for camp. Certainly it is a major camp fad. One should be cautious, though, and recall that, for all its elements of seeming ambiguity and parody, Mannerism must properly be situated in the context of the spirituality, sensitivity and idealism of the High Renaissance. Many Mannerist paintings that seem camp when set in the wider frame of the twentieth century, seem much less so when put back

The Madonna with the Long Neck by Parmigianino.

William Beckford, whom J.G. Lockhart called 'a male Horace Walpole'—perhaps an unfair aspersion on Beckford's sexuality.

in the sixteenth century. Much of Mannerism is closer in mood to the monumental and most-definitely-not-camp achievements of Renaissance Italy than it is to the work of an artist like Beardsley, which we can call camp with total confidence.

Learning, which the sixteenth century saw spreading though the secular world, helped to produce the self-consciousness which is a *sine qua non* of camp—books, like mirrors, are gateways to detachment. Camp exploited the new learning in a characteristically idiosyncratic way. Cerebral, but on the whole uninterested in the great questions of philosophy or science, it aspires to erudition rather than wisdom. Its preoccupation with style and its aspiration towards sophistication demand only a nodding acquaintance with many different areas of culture and social history. Although Angus Wilson has recorded the existence of Senior Common Room Camp, the attractions of learning have on the whole been its decorative aspects rather than the labour of serious study.

In the fields of art and literature, camp's far-reaching but unintegrated learning is reflected in its eclecticism. Mannerism, as described by Vasari, copied the most beautiful objects in Renaissance paintings and joined them together synthetically in an attempt to create the greatest possible beauty. Ludwig II's castles combined the Rococo, Gothic, Byzantine, Romanesque and Moorish. In modern times, Pop artists, such as Marcel Duchamp's disciple, Richard Hamilton, have made much use of collage, juxtaposing images from films, magazines and advertising posters with more painterly effects. And, as both Peter York in *Style Wars* and Dick Hebdige in *Subculture: the Meaning of Style* have noted, punk's pastiche clothing transfers the collages of Pop art from canvas to the human body.

But perhaps the most common manifestation of camp erudition over the past two centuries has been the habit of collecting. This was traditionally a feminine pastime and was parodied as such by Pope's contemporary John Gay:

> 'What ecstasies her bosom fire!
> How her eyes languish with desire!
> How blest, how happy should I be,
> Were that fond glance bestow'd on me!
> New doubts and fears within me war:
> What rival's near? A *China* Jar.'

Subsequently, though, collecting was taken up by camp men. Beau Brummell, Robert de Montesquiou and Boni de Castellane (of whom more later) all had a passion for collecting beautiful objects. Perhaps the epitome of the camp collector, though, was William Beckford, whom Disraeli called 'the man of greatest taste'.

'I have never been over-fond of resisting temptation,' said Beckford's fictional alter ego, Vathek. Young boys presented a temptation which Beckford himself did not resist, with the result that he was excluded from the

Fonthill Abbey: a beacon of Beckford's megalomania.

Society into which he would otherwise have been welcomed because of his great wealth. He built a hideaway for himself in the shape of Fonthill Abbey, a huge folly mixing Gothic, Oriental and Spanish styles, with a tower taller than the steeple of Salisbury Cathedral. Inside this folly he amassed a huge collection of furniture, books and paintings. He had a high wall built around the grounds of the Abbey, became an almost total recluse, and devoted himself to his collection. Hazlitt said of him that he was 'an industrious *bijoutier*, a prodigious virtuoso, an accomplished patron of unproductive labour, an enthusiastic collector of expensive trifles,' while Fonthill was 'a desert of magnificence, a glittering waste of laborious idleness, a cathedral turned into a toyshop.'

Ironically, Beckford won more of the attention he craved by his well-advertised withdrawal from society than he ever did when he defied conventions within it. In the neighbourhood of Fonthill, rumours abounded concerning the orgies that were supposed to take place on the other side of the wall, the magic rituals and the troupes of dwarfs given to unnatural practices. And it was a mark of the campness of Beckford's temperament, that he played up to these rumours.

Of the arts, the theatre played a dominant rôle in glamourising insincerity, an essential ingredient of camp, encouraging its audiences to take the short step to a playful off-stage theatrical insincerity, and influencing them to view manners in a detached and ironic light. The Comedy of Manners then emerging, shifted the emphasis from moral dilemmas to stylistic ones—not 'What shall I do?' but 'What shall I wear?' According to the critic, Norman Holland, Restoration comedies were the first openly to recommend insincerity, as in Congreve's: '...a wit should no more be sincere than a woman constant: one argues a decay of parts, as t'other of beauty.' Wycherley argued the case at greater length:

'Why are harsh Statutes 'gainst poor Players made,
When Acting is the Universal Trade?
The World's but one wide Scene, our Life the Play
And ev'ry Man an Actor in his Way:
In which he, who can act his ill Part well,
Does him, who acts a good one ill, excell
Since it is not so much his Praise, whose Part
Is best, but His who acts it with most Art.'

The characters held up for admiration in Restoration comedies are those who dextrously and successfully manipulate their self-presentation for their own self-advancement; the characters we laugh at rather than with try to do the same, but make a mess of it. Clothes make-up, disguise, deceit, affectation, etiquette, pretence: all these acquired special meaning in the Restoration; they are also, of course, the paraphernalia of camp.

Laurence Olivier as Tattle in a 1965 production of William Congreve's *Love for Love*. 'What's here? Mrs Foresight and Mrs Frail? They are earnest—I'll avoid 'em.'

Pluralism (in the sense of adopting various personalities to deal with the contingencies of city life), the preoccupation with style, and the renaissance in learning were parallel tendencies in a much deeper and wider trend: the unprecedented growth of the middle classes in the sixteenth century. This was perhaps the most important single factor in the development of camp, because although a handful of early, prototypical figures lived and played in court and camp, the vast majority of camp people from Beau Brummell to Oscar Wilde, from William Congreve to Ronald Firbank, from Vincent Voiture to Andy Warhol, from Sarah Bernhardt to Mick Jagger, have sprung from and formed themselves in relation to the middle classes. Broadly speaking, camp developed in tandem with the bourgeoisie.

Since its literally noble beginnings, camp has needed a prosperous bourgeoisie, both because it presupposes an establishment to be marginal to and because it requires a society in which a superfluity of wealth can support its idleness. The separation of work and leisure provides camp both with something good and solid to defy and with a relatively carefree and frivolous arena in which to enjoy

53

itself. Camp regards itself as marginal to the world that
reveres industry, progress, convention, marriage and
respectability—all things that traditionally have been
upheld by the bourgeois male. It therefore accommodates
itself to an analysis similar to the modern feminist analysis
of the feminine. Camp people share not only a common
oppressor with feminists, but also a view of human
relationships as motivated by vanity, egotism and the will
to dominate, and they too interpret the human
personality primarily in sexual terms. However, one of
the paradoxes of the camp mentality is that, while it
defines itself primarily in sexual terms, it is usually
asexual.

In 1943, Simone de Beauvoir described the traditionally
feminine woman as an incidental being, frivolous,
infantile and irresponsible. Femininity, she revealed, is an
artful construct imposed on a woman, rather than a purely
spontaneous expression of her individuality. In 1963,
Betty Friedan called femininity a form of immaturity: the
feminine woman is frivolous, childlike and fluffy—not
involved. Having no real purpose or opportunity for
achievement, she becomes a mere faddist, a marginal
creature not sharing in the whole of human destiny.
Excluded from humanity's greater concerns, she is left
only with its trivia. In 1964, Elizabeth Janeway
specifically developed the analogy between woman and
the effeminate homosexual: both are forced by the
prejudices of heterosexual men 'to accept one aspect of
themselves, their sexuality, as isolating them and
opposing them to the norms of society.' Pushed in on

Traditionally Feminine Woman:
Jayne Mansfield being domesticated
in Frank Tashlin's *The Girl Can't
Help It* (1956).

themselves, they become narcissists. The customary attitude towards them makes them 'veer away from participation in the most advanced and progressive side of our activist, scientific culture, even to deny that they are interested in it or likely to be competent at it.' They are separated from the use of power. Homosexuals, she says, 'are lumped together by the large and simplistic assumption that if they don't act entirely as men, there's only one thing they can be: some sort of sham woman.' Germaine Greer (1970) describes how 'in their clothes and mannerisms women caricature themselves, putting themselves across with silly names and deliberate flightiness, exaggerating their indecisiveness and helplessness, faking all kinds of pretty tricks.' Kate Millet (1971) talks of how camp men ape feminine women. She complains that women's (and, by implication, camp men's) thoughts are pushed on to a 'generally trivial or ephemeral plane'; women are 'customarily deprived of any but the most trivial sources of dignity and self respect.' They 'develop group characteristics common to those who suffer minority status and a marginal existence': they are forced into accommodating tactics, assuming an air of helplessness and making 'comic statements of deference': they become 'decorous nonentities'.

The feminist analysis seems to touch on camp at all points. The intellectual barriers between feminists and camp people have been broken down, the hostile arguments trampled underfoot. The feminists seem to be cornered—will they have to capitulate to camp? No! At

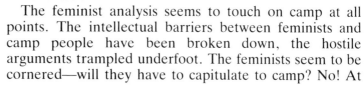

Left: Bette Davis in Robert Aldrich's 1962 film, *What Ever Happened to Baby Jane?* to which the advertising slogan answered: 'She grew some.' *Right:* In the pink—Barbara Cartland, voluminous Romantic novelist.

Oscar Wilde by 'Ape'. 'What on earth should we men do going about with purity and innocence? A carefully thought-out buttonhole is much more effective.'

the last minute, there is a cavalry charge by good, old-fashioned prejudice, which saves the day. Despite the nominal kinship between feminists and homosexuals, feminists off-guard exhibit a hatred of male homosexuals (at least camp ones). To take a blatant example, when Germaine Greer wants a vividly descriptive phrase to bring home the state of utter desperation into which woman has been manoeuvred, she calls her a 'female faggot'.

The fact is that while feminism and camp may share the same point of departure, they travel in different directions.

The feminist pose is heroic where camp's is unserious and self-depreciating. Feminists seek to abolish or to minimise their marginal status, while the camp try to make a virtue of marginality. Where feminism uses polemic, camp relies on mockery—something about which most feminists hold the gravest suspicions.

All his life, the camp person remains a naughty child cheeking his elders. The targets of this mockery—conventional morality, good taste, marriage and the family, suburbia, sport and business—should help to throw the camp personality into relief.

Conventional morality has always been an easy target for mockery. In a society with no conventional morality, if such a thing is conceivable, there could be no camp. There must be bounds of moderation to cross. Camp is a protest born out of satiety with convention: its wit loves to contradict the platitudinous strictures and comfy maxims of the Silent Mediocrity.

'Strength of conscience proceeds from weakness of purse.' (Sir John Vanburgh)

'There is no harm in any pursuit, provided it does not injure the figure.' (Thomas Lister)

'A little sincerity is a dangerous thing, and a great deal is absolutely fatal.' (Disraeli)

'Routine keeps one within the limits of mediocrity.' (Boni de Castellane)

'There is only one sin, and that is stupidity.' (Wilde)

'My needs are simple, admittedly, but such as they are they have all been satisfied over and over again.' (Cedric in Nancy Mitford's *Love in a Cold Climate*.)

'If I'm faced with a choice between two evils, I always like to choose the one I haven't tried before.' (Mae West)

'I *do* like my enemies, but only in the hope that it will aggravate them further.' (Jean Cocteau)

Good taste, the aesthetic equivalent of conventional morality, gets similarly short shrift:

'Nothing is really beautiful unless it is useless; everything useful is ugly. The most useful place in a house is the lavatory.' (Gautier)

'A whimsical goddess [i.e. Art] and a capricious, her strong sense of joy tolerates no dulness [*sic*], and, live we never so spotlessly, still may she turn her back on us.

'As, from time immemorial, she has done upon the Swiss in their mountains.

'What more worthy people! Whose every Alpine gap yawns with tradition, and is stocked with noble story: yet, the perverse and scornful one will none of it, and the sons

James McNeill Whistler by Max Beerbohm. Whistler adopted the butterfly as his signature and as the symbol of his anti-utilitarian view of Art. Of his own times, he complained, 'Humanity takes the place of Art, and God's creatures are excused their usefulness. Beauty is confounded with virtue, and, before a work of Art, it is asked: "What good shall it do?"'

of patriots are left with the clock that turns the mill, and the sudden cuckoo, with difficulty restrained in its box!' (James McNeill Whistler)

'Good taste is the enemy of good art.' (Marcel Duchamp)

'The height of elegance is to create harmony in bad taste.' (Jean Genet)

Camp subverts conventional morality and taste not just with epigrams and persiflage, but with the whole camp 'performance'. More than just a mental tic, the spirit of

Mae West, irresistible as always, in *She Done Him Wrong* (1933).

perversity possesses the camp person's whole being. It is often suggested that the 'performance' mimics the sexual stereotypes that are the building bricks of patriarchal morality, not only to point to the faults in bad originals, but also in such a way as to draw attention to their arbitrariness. The cross-sexual camp burlesque, then, shows how easily sexual stereotypes could be otherwise: that it is not an immutable law of the universe that men should be macho and women feminine, that it would take only a little injection of levity to throw the system of social stereotypes into disarray. After watching Mae West or a drag queen, we should feel less inclined to take, for example, coquettishness seriously—more detached from the rituals of courtship in which we are expected to participate. The power of sex roles to restrict us is in theory diminished.

Camp mockery also attacks relationships between the sexes more directly, particularly where marriage and the family are concerned. Camp men, confronted with the possibility of marriage, are likely to worry, perhaps as Monsieur did when he first saw his wife to be—a bloated blonde in the Teutonic style—that they might not be able to manage. The camp male is a sexually ambiguous drone whose recurrent nightmare is that some woman will force him to take liberties with her; he shrinks from the drudgery of marital sex, identifying it with 'the daily grind'. Marriage is unpopular with the camp because it combines the maximum temptation with the maximum disinclination to be tempted. Proximity compels sincerity, and the camp bachelor or spinster must be free to enjoy the vertiginous exhilarations of insincerity.

Nowhere is this predicament better dramatised than in the 'Lucia' novels of E.F. Benson—which are like camp P.G. Wodehouse. These stories take place in charming little villages of olde worlde houses with leaded lattice windows and oak beams. The inhabitants are dedicated to cultural activities of the order of piano playing (generally the 'Moonlight' sonata), watercolour sketching (works with titles like 'Roses of Summer' or 'Golden Autumn Wonderland'), needlework, bridge and yoga. The resident drone is Georgie Pilson, a 'not obtrusively masculine sort of person', who is very proud of a collection of *bibelots* that are generally understood to have been bequeathed, 'though the inheritance had chiefly passed to him through the media of curiosity shops.' To press the Wodehouse analogy to its limits, the other two major characters are the two 'aunt' figures, Lucia herself ('Aunt Dahlia') and the more overtly dangerous Miss Mapp ('Aunt Agatha').

They live in a constant fever of pretension. When Lucia first moves into her cottage, 'The Hurst', and discovers that

Hinge and Bracket in their own television show, affectionately mocking the solid good taste of the bourgeoisie.

the genuine Elizabethan front door is falling apart, she has the village blacksmith construct another one, studded with large iron nails of antique pattern, some of them arranged to look as if they might spell AD 1603.

Few tourists leave Miss Mapp's (neighbouring) village of Tilling without buying a Tilling moneybox in the form of a pottery pig. Miss Mapp 'had a long shelf full of these [pigs] in every colour to adorn her dining room. The one which completed her collection, of a pleasant magenta colour, had only just been acquired. She called them "my sweet rainbow of piggies" and often when she came down to breakfast, especially if Withers (her maid) was in the room, she said "Good morning, quaint little piggies." When Withers left the room she counted them.'

The plots of these books concern the constant struggle for domination of the local cultural life that keeps these two viragos up to the mark, and the misfortunes of the wispy Georgie as he is tossed lightly between them.

E.F. Benson is a master of the Bourgeois Macabre. Other leading exponents of the genre include Saki, whose ephebic heroes, like Georgie, spend much of their time trying to escape the clutches of various bossy women, and John Betjeman, that celebrated lambaster of 'chintzy, chintzy cheeriness'.

In his *Memoirs of an Aesthete*, Harold Acton describes how he and Brian Howard (Evelyn Waugh's model for Anthony Blanche in *Brideshead Revisited* and Ambrose Silk in *Put Out More Flags*) used to walk from Eton into Slough on Sunday afternoons. There, in the suburbs, they sought hints of flagellation and black magic behind the apparently respectable façade. They marvelled at women with hatpins who looked as if they would carry sexual rapacity to the point of cannibalism. Out of these walks came the short story *Baroness Ada*, which Brian Howard contributed to a school magazine, the *Eton Candle*, published in 1922. On a dreary Sunday in the suburbs of Aldershot, a young man approaches a Victorian Gothic villa, and knocks on the door in order to request a cup of tea. He is conducted upstairs by a cockney governess ('mind the steps, dearie—lawks, the elastic has snapped on my slipper'), who takes him into the Baroness's bedroom. The Baroness greets him in a dressing gown. She has a voice of amazingly low pitch. The walls of the bedroom are lined with wardrobes packed with hundreds of costumes, dresses and petticoats. After some desultory conversation (the Baroness, it seems, is also a cockney), the governess and the Baroness suddenly jump on the young man, throw him on the bed and tear from the cupboards armfuls of clothes, with which, as the story ends, they set about smothering him.

Camp finds something awfully funny about the musty respectability of suburbia—the pebble-dashed semis with their differentiated bays and peacock windows; the world

The genially spiteful Australian matron, Dame Edna Everage, alias Barry Humphries.

of fish fingers, biscuit tins, Sweetex, day-trips, clipped hedges and ducks on the wall (other-worldly yearnings infinitely vulgarised), of hankies, cardies and daffs, of bijoux baronial halls (three up and three down) with the reproductions of *The Hay Wain* favoured by those who would like to have sporting prints, but don't feel they could carry it off, of women who dream about having the Queen round to tea, and then in discussion, over coffee, the next morning, say, 'I wouldn't have *her* job.'

The idea of the suburb as a camp fad was popularised in the 1960s by Joe Orton, in whose black comedies the net-curtained hypocrisy of petit-bourgeois England is repeatedly flicked aside to offer glimpses of horrifying depravity: 'I shall accompany my father to Confession this evening. In order to purge my soul of this afternoon's events,' says a character in *Loot*. 'Afterwards I'll take you to a remarkable brothel I've found. Really remarkable. Run by three Pakistanis aged between 10 and 15. They do it for sweets. Part of their religion.'

Boarding schools, those great power houses of bourgeois mentality, are another natural target for camp mockery. Schoolboy adventure books have long been camp fads, but for pure camp we turn to Arthur Marshall's stories about girls' boarding schools, which parody those of Angela Brazil, as in this passage about a

The most popular member of Britain's suburban royal family: the Queen Mother waving to crowds outside Clarence House on her 78th birthday.

headmistress appearing for an exhibition boxing match in front of the whole school:

'A gaze-compelling figure in roomy maroon shorts, her torso snugly housed in a cerise zephyr, she had trained down to the promising weight of thirteen stone ten, and an exciting little burst of shadow-boxing before she went to her corner revealed the tiger. Serenely confident, she was recalling her undergraduette days as a trim welter, and stood gently flexing her giant biceps and easing the sizeable thigh-sinews.'

The whipping/caning/birching aspect of boarding school life is an obvious target for camp humour, and camp people have never shrunk from the obvious: 'Algernon's bottom and Birkenshaw's rod/Ain't they a couple of lovers by God.' (Algernon Swinburne, *The Flogging Block*.

School games, the sort associated with sweat-encrusted woollen socks, with wet towels flicking spotty thighs, with persevering pluck and manly tussles have long been instillers of the anti-camp virtues of the bourgeoisie. Vyvyan Holland, Oscar Wilde's son, was all the more surprised, then, one day in Oxford, to come across the limp-wristed future novelist, Ronald Firbank, wearing a sweater and football shorts. He asked him what on earth he had been doing.

'Oh football.' he replied.
'Rugger or soccer?'
'Oh, I don't remember.'
'Well, was the ball round or egg-shaped?'
'Oh! I was never near enough to it to see that!'

Finally among the targets for camp mockery is the business in which other people have had to engage to keep the camp idle. 'Only insects and city people are busy,' said Brummell, and someone who asks Bulwer Lytton's Pelham if he has a watch provokes this magnificent tirade:

' "Watch!" said I, "Do you think I could ever wear a watch? I know nothing so plebian: what can anyone, but a man of business who had nine hours for his counting house and one for his dinner, ever possibly want to know the time for? An assignation, you will say, true: but (here I played with my best ringlet) if a man is worth having, he is surely worth waiting for." '

Camp people generally dread a steady job. If they must work they usually try to do so in idleness-related industries, or in a business nicely tinged with art, so that they can at least console themselves that theirs is not a

Above: Ronald Firbank at Chamonix, 1916. This camp novelist was said to have the most wicked laugh in London.

Georgia Sitwell photographed by Cecil Beaton, 1927.

proper job. In the seventeenth century, the playwrights tell us, camp people tended to work on the stage or as pimps. At the turn of the century, Baroness Elsie Deslandes was a notorious beauty who greeted her guests lying beneath her portrait by Burne-Jones, on a bed of lilies, and feeding her bronze tortoise with jewels: her only work was posing for paintings. Nowadays, camp people are often associated with entertainment, fashion or interior decoration.

Camp people like to give the impression that they are blithely oblivious to economic realities.

'I am fond of work,' says Lady Marney in Disraeli's *Sybil*, 'and I talk always about it.'

'Ah! You are fortunate,' replies Lady de Mowbray, 'I never could work; and Joan and Maud, they neither of them work. Maud did embroider a banner once... I think it beautiful: but somehow or other she never cultivated her talent.'

The materialistic philosophy, utilitarianism, was dubbed brutalitarianism by Disraeli, and when Wilde said, 'All art is absolutely useless,' he meant that all good art was absolutely anti-utilitarian, though that wouldn't have danced off the tongue quite so daintily.

The notions of 'getting on' and 'making good' and 'doing well for oneself' are anathema to the camp person who does not so much put his best foot forward as his best

Opposite: Cecil Beaton at home, 1934.

65

LASSITUDE

Robe de diner, de Paul Poiret

A Dandy Fainting or An Exquisite in Fits by George Cruikshank—there is an element in camp that shrinks from the heat of life.

leg, and that for the purposes of display rather than propulsion.

A major trait in camp self-presentation is boredom. Thin and delicate like Brummell, camp people are crushed to the ground by time, or fat and indolent like Prinnie, they find each minute barely wide enough for them to squeeze through. Camp exists in an environment in which the threat is not material want but boredom, a phenomenon that in camp's luxurious detachment swells into lush and convoluted forms of lassitude.

A character in Thomas Love Peacock's *Nightmare Abbey* (1818) complains 'Heigho! Laughter is pleasant, but the exertion is too much for me.' In Ronald Firbank's *The Flower Beneath the Foot*, Her Dreaminess the Queen tells her son to take her earrings off, because they are tiring her out. And when Brian Howard felt he needed some exercise, he used to send for someone to cut his hair, after which exertion he would have to lie down 'for simply hours'.

A camp quality of voice may also express lassitude: the typical diction is slow almost to the point of expiration, with heavy emphasis on inappropriate words (lots of capital letters and italics) rising painfully to a climax, to be followed by a series of swift cadences—a sort of rollercoaster effect, which in Regency times was known as the 'drawing room drawl'.

Concomitant with camp boredom is delicacy. Brummell said that he had caught a cold because he had been 'left in a room with a damp stranger', and Beardsley suffered a

Opposite: Lassitude by Paul Poiret. 'We spend out lives,' said Thomas Lister, 'in conjugating the verb "*je m'ennuie*".'

similar affliction because he accidentally left a tassel off his cane. 'Riding' said Bulwer Lytton's Pelham, 'is too severe an exercise for me, it is only fit for the robuster nerves of women—will any gentleman present lend me his essence bottle?' Delicate nerves in camp women are often suggested indirectly through their highly-strung pet dogs: there are few more magnificent sights than a big lady with a pack of poodles, their leads radiating out from her like guy-ropes, each creature being nothing more or less than a bundle of nerve fibres on legs.

In seventeenth-century France, Pascal argued that man's only consolation in a life of otherwise unremitting boredom was to channel his energies into *divertissements*. Among them, he suggests vanity, the pleasures of showing off, and dancing. The camp might have taken their cue from Pascal: carnivals, fêtes, salons, masked balls, fashion parades, nightclubs, bars, discos, and

Opposite: Mrs Mosscockle, photographed by Cecil Beaton who wrote of her in *The Wandering Years*: 'Today, Rita Mosscockle must be pushing eighty. She looks like a macabre travesty of Queen Alexandra. In fact, some Eton boys actually think Rita is a reincarnation of the Rose Queen and, to her delight, they take off their hats when she drives through Windsor in her carriage.'

Above: The Ypres Ball, November 1922. Princess Astafieva (with boa) and pupils. *Left: The Rocky Horror Picture Show* (1975), which guys the conventions of both the horror movie and the musical. Richard Dyer has claimed that horror movies appeal to the camp because of a fascination with the disguising of depravity as normality.

69

parties—they have almost made these forms of social organisation their own; only in these activities do camp people unfold and feel free; mutual support and admiration inspires them with the confidence to give full vent to their passions for exhibitionism, scandal, luxury and self-decoration. At parties, camp people can be themselves, which is to say, whoever they want to be.

Parties have never seemed more magnificent (or more camp) than in the pages of *A La Recherche du Temps Perdu*: Marcel Proust wrote some delightfully camp Comedy of Manners, but unfortunately he kept on spoiling it by drifting into a dreary Pateresque neo-platonism (the worst kind, my dear), becoming too introspective to be considered properly camp. The character around whom most of the lighter and camper aspects of the novel revolve is Baron de Charlus, who was based on Robert de Montesquiou, Proust's friend until the publication of the book.

'He meanwhile was posted between the house and the garden, by the side of the German Ambassador, leaning upon the balustrade of the great staircase which led from the garden to the house, so that the other guests...were obliged to greet him as they passed. He responded by naming each of them in turn... This created a continuous barking sound interspersed with benevolent suggestions or inquiries (to the answers to which he paid no attention), which M. de Charlus addressed to them in a tone softened, artificial to shew his indifference, and benign: "Take care the child doesn't catch cold, it is always rather damp in the gardens... Good evening, Madame de Mecklembourg. Have you brought your daughter? Is she wearing that delicious pink frock?"'

Portrait of the Marquis de Castellane after a drawing by Briant. 'A little disdain is not amiss, a little scorn is alluring.' (Congreve).

De Montesquiou's biographer, Philippe Jullian, has said of him that he had a genius for parties, and they have certainly remained a by-word in camp circles since. They are mentioned, for example, in Nancy Mitford's *Love in a Cold Climate*. Parties, said de Montesquiou, should always be given *against* someone, and when he was drawing up a list of *invités* for a party, he also used to draw up a long list of *excludés* which was equally well-publicised. His *invités* sometimes included his friend Whistler, and sometimes Sarah Bernhardt, with whom he had a brief and inconclusive affair. One famous celebration centred on the installation at de Montesquiou's house at Neuilly of a bath made out of ten tons of pink marble, which was said to have been given by Louis XV to Madame de Pompadour. The poetess Anna de Noailles addressed poems to it. It is difficult to divine what it is about the idea of this bath that is intrinsically amusing. Perhaps it is that one suspects that Madame de Pompadour herself might have looked as if she were made of ten tons of pink marble.

Above: Boni de Castellane at a fancy dress ball as the Marshall of Saxony. The lavishness of his parties led contemporaries to speculate that he had more money at his disposal than Louis XIV. *Right:* Robert de Montesquiou *à la japonaise*.

Boni de Castellane, said by his aunt to walk as if he had peacock feathers stuck in his bottom, was Robert de Montesquiou's great rival in extravagance. Though virtually penniless himself, he paid for his parties (which might involve 60 footmen, 80 ballet dancers, and 15 kilometres of carpet) with his wife's money. Someone had earlier said of this lady, a meaty American heiress, that she'd never be foolish enough to marry anyone who wanted to marry her, but obviously de Castellane somehow induced her to share in his prodigious conceit, for not only did she marry him, but for many years she seemed unable to deny him any requests for financial assistance.

Some incidents in his *Confessions* are reminiscent of Proust's Baron de Charlus passages. One keen socialite whom de Castellane determined not to invite to a particular party was Mrs Moore, another American woman with no sense of proportion—an affliction, he said, to which her body bore more adequate witness.

'We had not included Mrs Moore in our list of *invitées*, an omission which sorely troubled the good lady so much that she became positively ill with the complaint known as "hope deferred". At last, unable to endure the agony of suspense any longer, she rushed off to see my mother in whom she confided her woes. "My digestion is completely

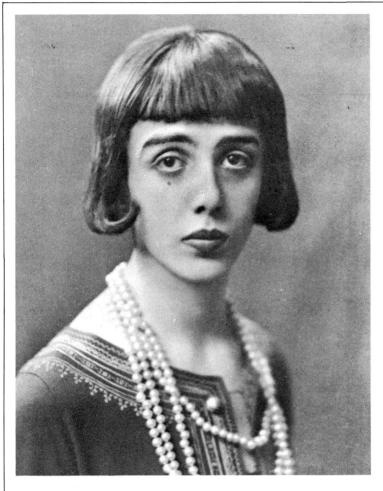

Brian Howard at Eton.

upset," she lamented, and my mother, who is the most amiable of women, touched by her distress, begged me to send Mrs Moore a belated invitation. This I did, hoping (to my shame) that she would not have time to arrange her fancy dress. But I had not reckoned with Mrs Moore—she had already provided herself with one weeks before, and she appeared in our ballroom as a guelder-rose.

'But what kind of guelder-rose? None with which our eyes were familiar! Mrs Moore looked more like a sugared Easter Egg than any rose, known or unknown! She carried a tall white walking stick *à la mode* de Louis XV, on the top of which a stuffed green parrot swayed to and fro. Her entrance was the signal for a general outburst of gaiety, and the Spirit of Carnival pervaded the dancers who joined hands, and romped round the guelder-rose, much to her delighted astonishment.'

What Beau Brummell was to the Regency and what Robert de Montesquiou was to the Belle Epoque, Brian Howard was to the Bright Young Things—a fount of inventive frivolity. Maddeningly irresponsible and adorably silly (in intention anyway), his set sped from

Opposite: an invitation to a party organised by Brian Howard.

72

THE GREAT URBAN DIONYSIA

THE DIONYSIA WILL OCCUR THIS YEAR

AT 1 MARYLEBONE LANE, OXFORD STREET

(BEHIND BUMPUS'S) ON THE 4TH OF APRIL 1929

AT 11 P.M., CELEBRATED BY

BABE PLUNKET GREENE

IN HONOUR OF THE TWENTY-FOURTH BIRTHDAY OF

BRIAN HOWARD

AND BECAUSE THE NEW ATHENS IS SORRY THAT

DAVID TENNANT

IS GOING TO ACADIA

Each guest must be dressed as a *definite* character in *Greek* mythology, and is bringing wine. Extraordinarily beautiful dresses, which are not expensive to make, may be copied with great ease from the Greek vases in the British Museum.

The accompanying card will admit you, and you alone. *Please do not forget to bring it with you.*

"Jeunes gens glacés des villes qui portez votre intelligence à côté de vous comme une canne, relisez cette *Lettre a Maritain* si mal, si vite lue, que vous avez prise pour une confession bruyante, alors que c'était un de ces cris du coeur où les doctrines n'ont que faire. N'entendez-vous pas crier dans les glaces? Ne voyez-vous pas cette preuve que Dieu exige toutes vos forces et tous vos scandales? Aimez, aimez, aimez, comme bon vous semble et quittez cet air fin qui paralyse les ailes et vous empêche de voler."

from " J'adore "
by
JEAN DESBORDES

"Jeunes gens qui m'écoutez, qui me regardez, qui me croyez, jeunes gens de partout, du vieux monde et du nouveau monde, je monte à un balcon en l'air qui domine les murs qu'on cherche à mettre entre nous, les mensonges et ma légende; je vous parle: ce livre enseigne l'anarchie nouvelle qui consiste à aimer Dieu sans limites, à perdre votre prudence et à dire tout ce qui vous passe par le coeur."

the concluding paragraph in
the Preface by
JEAN COCTEAU
to " J'adore "

J'ACCUSE

Intellect
No
Ladies and Gentlemen
Chic
Anglo-Catholics
Hicks
Public Schools
O.T.C.
Officers
Débutantes
Ascot and Lords
English " Society "
Those incredibly " Private "
Dances
The *Tatler* and the *Sketch*
The London Group
Masters Club
Orpen
Tell-tale-tits, slit-tongues, lickspittles and all social snippet writers
Sadist devotees of blood-sports
Keyserling
James Douglas the Bigot
People who still think that a title is of the slightest importance
Gertrude Stein
Bowler hats, the gravestones of charm
People who find themselves out of place in a full third-class carriage anywhere in the world
Missionaries
John Bull, Blunt and all the rest of that ranting, canting rot
Le Touquet
" Eligible bachelors "
The Spectator
The Fortnightly Review
Hodder & Stoughton
People who dislike going to pubs
Elgar
People who say they can't meet so-and-so because " they've got such a bad reputation, MY DEAR "
Belloc
The sort of young men one meets at great, boring, sprawling tea-parties in stuck-up, moronic country houses, who say, whenever anyone else says, at last, anything worth saying: " Well, I prefer Jorrocks " and snort into their dung-coloured plus-drawers
Inge
The Bright Young People
Melton
All those people with faces like forks who roar about " bad form "
People who confuse nakedness with indecency
Sir Reginald Blomfield
Nationalism

J'ADORE

Intuition
Yes
Men and Women
Elegance
Love
Plato
Charles Chaplin
Robert Bridges
The Crystal Palace
Nietzsche
Lily Morris
Picasso
Wild Flowers
Eluard
Tennyson
Acrobats
Duveen
Mathias Grünewald
Boxing
Kokoschka
American Food
Edison
Duncan Grant
Dionysos
Einstein
El Greco
Grass
Donne
Wood and Stone
Slevogt
Segrave
Germany
Stanley Spencer
Jazz
The Incas
Granville Barker
Lindbergh
Sherlock Holmes
Desbordes
Russian Films
Cocteau
The Mediterranean
Marianne Moore
Milton
Mary Wigman
Small Islands
D. H. Lawrence
Beethoven
Stravinsky
The British Museum
A Field-mouse in a Bonnet
Schubert
Diaghilev
Montaigne
Havelock Ellis
Dornier Superwal
Norman Douglas
Greek Vases
Spengler
The sort of people who enjoy life just as much, if not more, after they have realised that they have not got immortal souls, who are proud and not distressed to feel that they are of the earth earthy, who do not regard their body as mortal coils, and who are not anticipating, after death, any rubbishy reunion, apotheosis, fulfilment, OR ANY THING

party to party: from bottle party to Venetian party, from masked party to pool party, from stunt party to punt party, from a fruit party to an impersonation party, and from a pedicure party to a bring-a-bank-statement party. Commitment to frivolity brought with it a revival of various accomplishments redolent of the salons of the seventeenth century: the composition of elaborately humorous invitations, comic poems (*vers de société*) and songs, short verbal portraits and/or mimicry of fellow guests.

In the affectionately mocking *Where Engels Fears to Tread*, published in his collection of essays called *The Condemned Playground*, Cyril Connolly, Howard's contemporary at Eton, captured his personal style. The Howard character is called Christian de Clavering:

'Parties! "Are you going to de Clavering's tonight?" and woe betide the wretch who had to say no. Nothing much happened at the time, but he soon felt he was living on an icefloe, drifting farther and farther from land, and every moment watching it melt away. De Clavering's to-night! The candles burn in their sconces. The incense glows. Yquem and Avocado pears—a simple meal—but lots and lots of both. "Have a brick of caviare, Alvanley? More birds' nest, Gleneagles? There's nothing coming, I'm afraid, only Avocado pear and hot-pot." "Hot-pot!" "Christian you're magnificent!" "Caviare and hot-pot—Prendy will be blue with envy!" And then dancing...'

Weaving its way around camp parties is scandal. If a camp person needs to be looked at when visible, he expects to be talked about when out of sight. He will often go to extraordinary lengths to render himself the subject of speculation; as Cocteau wrily remarked, 'Nothing is harder to keep up than a bad reputation.'

Many camp works of art aim at a *succès de scandale*. Some camp novels, such as Disraeli's *Vivian Grey* and Carl Van Vechten's *Peter Whiffle: his life and works* are *romans à clef* containing scurrilous portraits of people in public life. The plots of a significantly large proportion of camp plays and novels turn on scandal or the possibility of scandal. The supremely camp novels of Ronald Firbank proceed by hints, allusions, innuendos, indiscretions and eavesdroppings, myriad sexual perversions always seem to be taking place off-stage, with titters, the rustling of tulle and the whisperings of flesh against flesh. The very title of the novel *Inclinations*, gives an indication of the paramountcy of scandal in Firbank's scheme of things:

'Who exactly is she?'
'She's a pupil of Tasajara, Gerald.'
Miss O'Brookomore's nose grew long.

Camp noses have been considerably lengthened by Kenneth Anger's book of film star scandal, *Hollywood*

Opposite: Alla Nazimova in the film of Oscar Wilde's *Salomé* (1922), with designs inspired by Aubrey Beardsley.

Ramon Novarro *(left)* and Rudolph Valentino *(right)*.

Babylon, which contains tit-bits about many camp favourites including Gloria Swanson, Marlene Dietrich, Mae West, Lupe Velez, Lana Turner and Judy Garland ('Amphetamine Annie'). Anger gossips about, for example, the exotic lesbian actress Alla Nazimova and her Beardsley-inspired production of Wilde's *Salomé* acted exclusively by homosexuals, and the news that when Ramon Novarro, male sex symbol of the silent screen, was found dead in 1968, thrust down his throat was a black Art Deco dildo which had been given to him and signed in silver by Rudolph Valentino.

'I have Social Disease,' wrote Andy Warhol in *Exposures*. 'I have to go out every night. If I stay home one night, I start spreading rumours to my dogs. Once I stayed home for a week and my dogs had a nervous breakdown.' A timid man, Warhol used to give the impression of a sort of twentieth-century Lady of Shalott, unable to look at life directly, but only at its reflection on a television screen; nowadays he is a full-time socialite. His interest in camp gossip and scandal finds an outlet both in *Exposures* which he wrote (and which contains portraits of among others, Truman Capote and Diana

Opposite: David Bailey and Patrick Litchfield's magazine, *Ritz*. 'Scandal', said Saki, 'is merely the compassionate allowance which the gay make to the humdrum.'

No. 38 Feb. 1980

Bailey and Litchfield's

Price 50p ($2.00 800Yen)

RITZ
Newspaper

Andy Warhol Amanda Lear Amanda Grieve 3 Degrees

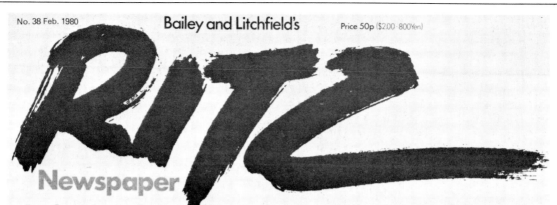

Vreeland, the *grande dame* of *Vogue*) and in *Interview* magazine, which he publishes. *Interview* consists largely of taped interviews with well-known and not-so-well-known personalities. Like Warhol's films, these interviews seem to lack direction and editing: the personality is simply encouraged to perform and the reader to eavesdrop. Much of what result is trivial, but then, of course, that is partly the point.

The camp person is, perhaps, too self-obsessed, too dazzled by his own persona ever fully to appreciate the glories of nature. The typically camp person (shall we call him Truman?) never looks at anything without seeing himself in it; Truman is there in the branches of the forest on a wild and windy night. Truman frolics with the lambs in the meadows: when Truman walks down a country lane every sparrow, every lark cries back to him 'Truman!' and when, on unsteady legs (for legs, out of courtesy, we must call them), Truman staggers out under a wide, starlit sky, who is that peering down from the moon (stands back aghast)—it is Truman!

George Brummell, described by Bulwer Lytton as 'the autocrat of the great world of fashion and cravats—the mighty genius before whom aristocracy hath been humbled and *ton* abashed—at whose nod the haughtiest *noblesse* of Europe had quaked...whose coat and whose friend were cut with an equal grace.'

Camp people are born in a Hall of Mirrors and never find their way out of it. Their lives are a lot happier, then, if their reflections are flattering; if not, they may, in their vanity, muse with Cocteau that 'mirrors ought to reflect longer before they return our images.' The camp encourage mirrors to be more thoughtful by their self-decoration.

A man who arrived at the foot of the stairs in Beau Brummell's house, was confronted by the valet coming downstairs with a tray of some twenty crumpled cravats: 'These are our failures,' said the valet. What is slightly less well-known is that in hommage to Brummell, the publisher Stockwell was moved to bring out a pamphlet: *Necklothitania or Tietania: Being an Essay on Starches*; he wrote, for instance, of the different possible styles of neck cloth:

'The Oriental is made with a *very* stiff and rigid cloth. Not a single indenture or crease should be visible. The Mathematical is far less severe. There are three creases in it. The colour best suited to it, is that called *couleur de la cuisse d'une nymphe émue*. The *Trône d'Amour* is well starched, with one single horizontal dent in the middle: colour, *Yeux de fille en extase*.'

Others of Brummell's sartorial extravagances included having three hairdressers: the first for his temples, the second for the front of his head and third for the back. Likewise, he employed two people to make his gloves, one making only the thumbs. When an aspiring young dandy asked how he made his boots shine so brilliantly, he replied, 'For blacking I never use anything but the froth of champagne.'

For sheer committment in this line, the Regency dandies were perhaps upstaged by the method devised by a certain mid-nineteenth century French baron to get a perfect shine on his silk hat. He made his valet run for half an hour every morning in the Bois de Boulogne. The baron's coachman then took the sweat off the valet's brow with a fine silk handkerchief and polished the hat with it. The important point though, was that the valet should be a clean, healthy boy, as blond as possible, because not all sweat would do.

Anyone who, as a child, has secretly dressed up in grown-ups' clothes and posed in front of a mirror—which is suddenly replete with dangerous possibilities, disclosing a wondrous, adult creature—can understand the camp preoccupation with toilette. Anyone who once knew the thrill of getting out the dressing-up box can understand how dressing-up in company invites others to enter into a game of make-believe and pretence which offers the chance of being more vividly alive.

It is common human experience that our clothes have a greater say in our personalities than we do: put on boots that make a nice loud clunk and we become bold and

Aubrey Beardsley's original of *The Toilette of Salomé*. 'The first duty in life is to be as artificial as possible,' said Wilde. 'What the second duty is no one has yet discovered.'

swaggering: cram our pillowy flesh into a tight cuirass of leather and we become lean and predatory. Put on sandals, and we are instantly castrated. Put on fancy dress and we can act out our wildest fantasies.

Perhaps, in the end, it is something sexual that fascinates in fancy dress: it seems to sanction sexual licence. One thinks of Louis XIV slipping off into the crowds in a mask that hides a face disfigured by lust, of Lord Rochester dressing up in drag to seduce an innkeeper's wife. There is a story about Ludwig II, whose prime minister went to try to make him show public support for his fighting troops, and, being refused admission by flunkies, forced his way into the king's bedroom. There he discovered Ludwig with his friend Prince Taxis, dressed up as Barbarossa and Siegfried, camping around under an artificial moon.

A crusty old journalist in a right-wing magazine recently complained that camp people determine what we all wear and how we decorate our homes. And indeed they are the leaders of fashion in these fields. As outsiders, they have been singularly successful in presenting themselves as insiders, operating a bluff which makes the merely marginal seem exclusive.

Camp's peculiar brand of snobbism regards itself not as a serious delineation of rightful social status, but as a good-humoured game. Of Trebeck, his fictionalised portrait of Brummell, Thomas Lister wrote, 'Nobody carried further that fashionable exclusiveness which prescribed the narrow limits of gentility and denounced all as Vandal beyond its bounds.' Brummell, the most snobbish and the most exclusive person in England was of lowly origin—his grandfather was a valet. Yet he did not try to hide this, because it was an essential part of the joke.

Now, as in Regency times, camp people maintain their exclusiveness by body-language, which can be used subtly to guy outsiders, by erudite references to camp culture and arcane fads, by in-jokes and by camp slang (e.g. naff, tat) ignorance of which would place a straight as Vandal.

Camp's cosmopolitan, cultural air is maintained by pidgin Italian and French (bona, glitterati, ignorati, la Swanson, les girls). Its habitual condescension is expressed in Hollywood cockney (pleased to meet yer, I'm sure... yer actual... I don't mind if I do). Coyness takes the form of baby talk (ducky, dolly) and in diminutives (bijou, the frequent use of the suffix -ette). Words that usually refer to women are applied to men (trolling, tarting up, frumpish, tomboyish) and male names have their genders changed (Georgina, Roberta). Displays of affection are usually larded with darlings and my dears, and a generally hyperbolic style conveys unabashed insincerity (too, too sick-making, frightfully unfunny, simply riveting). Theatrical slang plays a large part in camp vocabulary (making an entrance, upstaging). There is also a considerable stock of expressions of boredom and fastidiousness (bored beyond

Andrew Logan, director of the
Alternative Miss World competition.

measure, so very tiresome, can't abide, couldn't have been
more bored, inexpressibly bored). Camp language is at its
most inventive in the field of nicknames. The following are
from the novels of Jean Genet, the act of camp comedian
Larry Grayson, the 1981 Alternative Miss World contes-
tants and Beardsley's novel *Venus and Tannhäuser*: Notre
Dame des Fleurs, Mimosa, Mignon-les-petits-pieds, Apri-
cot Lil, Slack Alice, Miss Silicon Chip, Miss Potato, Miss
Aldershot, Little Cough-drop, Mrs Manly, Blessed Thing
and Trump.

Connected with camp exclusivism is the notion of divine
decadence. The camp love to see themselves as aristocrats
peeling a last grape while the barbarians outside are batter-
ing down the gates. '*Le dandysme apparaît surtout aux
époques transitoires où la démocratie n'est pas encore toute-
puissante, où l'aristocratie n'est que partiellement chance-
lante et avilie... Le dandysme est le dernier éclat d'héroisme
dans les décadences...un soleil couchant; comme l'astre qui
décline, il est superbe, sans chaleur et plein de mélancolie.*'
[Dandyisme appears above all during transitory epochs

when democracy is not yet all-powerful, when the aristocracy is just beginning to falter... Dandyism is the last splendour of heroism in decay...a setting sun, like a fading star, magnificent, but without heat and full of melancholy.] Although camp people often have a pseudo aristocratic style in their affected speech and artificial gestures—a relic perhaps of camp's origins—this quote from Baudelaire would make more sense as an expression of camp aspirations rather than as a frank appraisal of its place in society. Camp people have mostly been *arrivistes* (e.g. Brummell, Beckford, Disraeli and Firbank) who have despised their own class. They have perhaps identified themselves with the *précieux* poet Vincent Voiture, the son of a merchant, who was told by the nobleman who 'discovered' him: 'You are much too amusing to live among the bourgeoisie: I must pull you out of it.' Whistler called Wilde a *bourgeois malgré lui*. Camp people are

One of Jean Cocteau's drawings entitled *Le Mauvais Lieu*, which brilliantly catches the musty frissons of the camp bar.

generally examples of the bottom coming up, rather than the top coming down. If society is in decay, most camp people actually belong with the barbarians.

It might therefore be instructive to ask what the quint-essentially camp person and his opponent, the most stolid burgher, have in common. Like the lawman and the crim-inal, like the aesthete and the ascetic, they have a kinship of opposites.

Both are worldly and materialistic in the sense of being keen on acquiring nice possessions. Both are geared to success, though the camp person conceives success in terms of fame and the burgher more in terms of a constant accumulation of wealth. Generally speaking, pressing social problems make no more impression on the camp person than they do on the burgher. Both show a deliberate narrowness of intellect. The burgher is typically a self-made man and so, in another sense, is the camp person. Being self-assertive, both are to that extent unreceptive: the burgher, for instance, is as unappreciative of nature as the camp person: he is likely to drive out to picnic in the fields, then quickly decorate the landscape with brightly coloured cartons and rolled-up bits of tin foil to make it seem less alien. Both the camp person and the burgher have little love of the Church, unless it be for its element of show; both disregard its religious undertones. The quintes-sentially camp person deplores the fact that the burgher is so conventional, but then, of course, he is hardly less so himself.

Les Derniers Jours de Babylone by Rochegrosse accurately reflects the predilection of the camp to see themselves as decadents at the moment of the collapse of civilisation.

Mummy Is the Root of all Evil

Adolescence and exclusion. Vanity and self-hatred. Self-control and self-knowledge. Misanthropy. Misogyny and adoration. Bitchiness. Satiety. Display. Escapism. Duplicity and espionage. Shyness and exhibitionism. Pragmatism and happiness.

A striking feature of camp behaviour is that although it purports to be a coming out, an expression of individuality, camp people tend to be markedly similar. If every human being has a unique genetic blueprint, then the camp are not doing justice to that uniqueness in their self-presentation: they exemplify the rule that the more someone is a character, the less he is an individual. There is something literary or stagy about them, their movements are circumscribed by a limited number of stylised gestures, their voices are mannered, their vocabulary is notable for its reliance on stock phrases, and their cultural interests are confined to narrow margins of the mainstream. Everything they do is somehow second-hand: a camp person

Below: Vesta Tilley, a music hall performer who characteristically appeared in male dress. *Right:* Quentin Crisp, artist's model whose book, *The Naked Civil Servant,* turned him into a camp celebrity.

St Sebastian has long been a camp icon, symbolising, perhaps, the experience of ostracism. *Left:* the still from a poster advertising Derek Jarman's film with Latin dialogue, *Sebastiane*. *Opposite:* Eddy Marsh, impersonating St Sebastian *c*1912, from Julian Grenfell's *Games Book*, a personal pictorial diary.

boards a yacht like someone boarding a yacht, or arrives at a party like someone arriving at a party. What camp people gain in drawing a ready response to their witty and colourful nature, they lose in subtlety and complexity.

What obscure desire provokes a person to see his life merely as an opportunity for clowning, to submit to camp's oversimplification of the self, to exchange the fullness and depth of a portrait for the immediate but ephemeral pleasures of a caricature? Why should anyone efface his own individuality in order to adopt a secondhand persona and go through life at best as a harmless enthusiast, at worst as a music hall joke?

It is in adolescence that people seem particularly susceptible to the temptations of camp. The adolescent has to fashion his own personality, to begin shouldering burdens of maturity and, perhaps most difficult of all, to forge a sexual identity.

On the verge of adulthood, the adolescent looks at life as if at a play. His sense of incompatibility may turn in on itself so that he feels detached not only from life, but also from himself; sometimes he may feel so far detached that he would need to make a considerable leap of the imagination to sympathise with himself. Disillusioned and discouraged as he is, he is not up to that leap; he loses faith in feeling.

The natural disaffection of adolescence seems to grip some individuals with unnatural force. 'Excluded from the social order,' wrote Jean Genet in *The Thief's Journal*, 'I wondered at its perfect coherence, which rejected me. I was astounded by so rigorous an edifice whose details were united against me. Nothing in the world was irrelevant: the stars on a general's sleeve, the stock-market quotations, the olive harvest, the style of the judiciary, the wheat exchange, the flower beds... Nothing. This order, fearful and feared, whose details were all interrelated, had a meaning: my exile.' An intensified version of the feeling of marginality that is normal in adolescence can extend abnormally into adulthood. These individuals feel, perhaps in more senses than one, unequipped to perform the duties that are expected of them. The conventional mode of maturity is unable to go on, and camp is waiting in the wings.

The feelings of exclusion leading to camp are likely, if we may lob a conjecture back that far, to have begun in childhood. Growing up probably went awry at an early age. Knocked off balance in childhood, camp people never again get on an even keel, but swing from extreme to extreme. Edith Sitwell's childhood presents us with a compelling image of such suffering. Her parents, worried that she was disfigured, incarcerated her in a body-sized metal brace, a 'bastille of steel', in order to try, literally, to mould her into a normal child; it is no wonder that she attitudinised about her looks for the rest of her life. Sarah Bernhardt mentions repeatedly in her memoirs that she adored her mother, and no less often that her mother preferred her sister to herself. It is easy to see how this might have contributed to her lifelong drive to show off.

In modern folklore, the relationship which causes homosexual behaviour is that of a son to a bullying mother. In *Perversion, the Erotic Form of Hatred*, Robert Stoller neatly summarises the orthodox account: when the mother's relationship with the boy is too close and too blissful for too long, a disorder may develop in the boy out of rage at having to give up the relationship, out of panic that he will not be able to escape his mother's influence and out of a desire for revenge at her having put him in this predicament. Memoirs and biographies rarely probe deeply

Camp fad Rita Hayworth sings 'Put
the Blame on Mame!' in Charles
Vidor's *Gilda* (1944).

Gloria Swanson makes her exit, a star to the last, at the end of Billy Wilder's *Sunset Boulevard* (1950). She played an aged actress trying to make a comeback—a rôle that gave her full scope for the histrionic talents that have brought her a substantial camp following.

enough into infancy for us to test the relevance of this theory to camp. Nevertheless, we do know that Beckford, Beardsley, Wilde and Orton all had formidable mothers; other instances of this are evident in Miriam J. Benkowitz's biography of Ronald Firbank and Brian Howard's letters to his mother in *Portrait of a Failure*, which both show people locked into relationships with their mothers that are in some way abnormal and exclude them from normal relationships with others.

Feeling that the traditional modes of maturity are not for them, camp people commit themselves to various models of marginality. The Traditionally Feminine Woman, parodied in camp effeminacy, is the most obvious example. Camp uses femininity's connotations of flightiness, decorativeness, and so on. The other main models are: the Sexual Pervert, whose abnormalities are thought to exclude him from power and influence; the Sun King Courtier, a pampered apolitical figure with an elaborate and *outré* persona; the Ephebe, who is at the height of his physical attractiveness and zest and who is not yet weighed down by the burdens of responsibility (the camp, especially camp men, often retain a youthful appearance into old age); the Actor or Actress, who is devoted to display and who enjoys fame without power; and, most recently, the Film Star, who has superseded many of the functions both of the Sun King Courtier and the Actor/Actress, being apolitical, leisured, charismatic, physically beautiful and a

consumer of incomparable conspicuousness—nowadays the hip swing of Jayne Mansfield and the turned-up collar of Humphrey Bogart are plumes that camp people often borrow.

Since the ground of camp behaviour is a sense of exclusion, it may seem surprising that the most vaunted feature of camp performance should be its prodigious vanity—Vanbrugh's Lord Foppington says to his tailor, 'Aye, but let my people dispose the glasses so that I may see myself before and behind, for I love to see myself all raund.' Or there was Noel Coward who sent the Redgraves a silver wedding present of a photograph of Noel Coward gazing at a bust of Noel Coward and signed 'Noel Coward'. And there is this from Beardsley's *Venus and Tannhäuser*:

'After the chevalier got up, he slipped off his dainty night dress, posturing elegantly before a long mirror, and made much of himself. Now he would bend forward, now lie upon the floor, now stand upright, and now rest upon one leg and let the other hang loosely till he looked as if he might have been drawn by some early Italian master. Anon he would lie upon the floor with his back to the glass, and glance amorously over his shoulder. Then with a white silk sash he drapes himself in a hundred charming ways…'

Camp people preen themselves in public; vanity advertises itself in all their movements—it may be apparent, for example, in the effeminate way in which they splay their

Opposite: Noel Coward: diligent curator of his own legend.

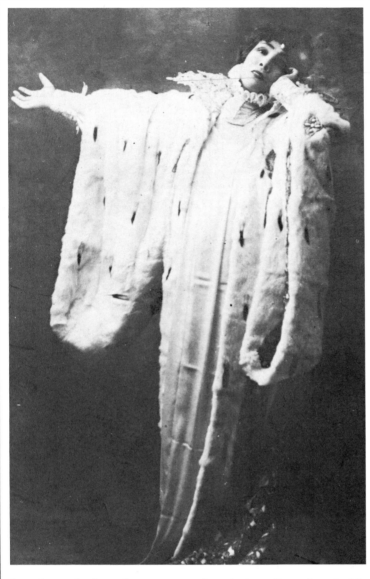

Sarah Bernhardt as Queen Elizabeth I of England: the look that says '*je m'adore*'.

hands out before them to examine their nails or in a habitual nervous crimping of hair behind the ears. Some camp people seem almost to languish with love of themselves. In fact, they may go to such extraordinary lengths to convince everyone that they find their own appearance adorable as to suggest that they protest too much.

With this suspicion swelling inside us we look again to representative camp people—Monsieur, Beardsley and Wilde—and we discover in them every possible disadvantage of feature and of limb. In fact, Wilde, with his thyroid eyes and lips not so much generous as profligate, was one of those people who are so ugly that even the most gentle and tender desire seems a monstrous depravity. Any narcissism here must have been grotesque, and any pretence to vanity, fraudulent. Perhaps the air of effort that hangs over some, at least, of camp vanity, may be accounted for by the fact that it is asserted against the odds. Vanity, then, may even be a means by which the camp person hides his own unattractiveness from himself.

Again, camp people behave as if they have been pampered and taught to think of themselves as the centre of the universe. When, in Thomas Lister's *Granby*, Lady Harriet is introduced to someone, she says: '...you will like me, I know—new people always do.' James McNeill Whistler sent Oscar Wilde a telegram on the day of the latter's wedding: 'Am detained. Don't wait.' Not only in its wit, but in its whole commitment to trivia, camp is heavily self-congratulatory.

But again, we should be suspicious—there is something bitter in camp conceit, something touchy and quick to take offence.

It would be altogether surprising if camp's vanity did not falter and if it were not alloyed with weaker materials. When he places himself outside the frame of reference of the majority and resists the temptation to go thrusting forward into the future with his more robust contemporaries, the camp person must resign himself to losing the dignity that goes with universal respect. Thus the commonplace has its revenge on camp, for such a loss must inevitably colour a person's self-esteem. He pays dearly for his emancipation from bourgeois dreariness and conformity;

Below: 'Awfully Weirdly'—Oscar Wilde described Beardsley as having 'a face like a silver hatchet, with grass-green hair'. Painting by Walter Sickert. *Right:* the young Oscar Wilde. As an older man, he remarked, 'To win back my youth there is nothing I wouldn't do—except take exercise, get up early or be a useful member of the community.'

he sees himself with his enemies' eyes, believing them to be his own—small wonder that he must try hard to like himself. Camp self-love is securely grounded in self-hatred, from which flow two other elements—camp self-control and camp self-knowledge.

Distrusting spontaneity, the camp person always acts in a measured way. There is a certain deliberation in everything he does. Even the most everyday of gestures may be made into a production number; camp people commonly show great attention to detail—a characteristic strength of the weak.

Regency dandies would practise for hours taking a pinch of snuff before daring to negotiate that difficulty in public, and in Max Beerbohm's *Zuleika Dobson*, the Duke of Dorset is said to be without rival in Europe in the art of taking and lighting a cigarette. Ludwig II was once observed unawares on a country walk:

'Everything about him was so peculiar as to be almost grotesque…was theatrical…was totally abnormal. He had no idea that anyone was looking at him, so he was not acting a part or striving after effect and yet—what studied pose and gait, what calculation in every movement and every expression! The unnatural had become for him the natural. In spite of it being summer he was wrapped in a heavy winter coat. He did not walk as other men walk, but took the stage like an actor in a coronation procession from one of Shakespeare's historical plays, casting his thrown-back head first to right and then to left…and carrying his hat before him with sweeping gestures.' Feeling himself

Feeling himself balanced precariously above a chasm of universal opprobrium, the camp person is as carefully self-controlled as a tight rope-walker.

Incidental to this self-control is a tendency towards stiffness—something artificial, inorganic and angular—which is parodied in Cruikshank's cartoons of Regency dandies and also in this passage in *Pelham*:

Monstrosities of 1822, engraving by George Cruikshank, published in 1835.

' "Come and sit by me, Millington,' cried old Lady Old-town; "I have a good story to tell you of the Duc de—" Sir Henry, with difficulty, turned round his magnificent head and muttered out some unintelligible excuse. The fact was, that poor Sir Henry was not that evening *made* to sit down—he had only his *standing-up* coat on!'

Since camp people control their personalities so rigidly, since, indeed, their personalities are their own creations, it is only to be expected that they should know them thoroughly. They would agree with the sentiment expressed by one of Ivy Compton Burnett's characters:

' "Know thyself" is a superfluous injunction: one can't help knowing oneself, the thing is to stop others from finding out!'

Camp people's knowledge of their own foibles forms a line of defence: others cannot call them anything which they have not called themselves. They have already coped with the worst that might be inflicted on them—there may be something of this in all masochism, and an element of masochism in all camp.

The methodology of camp's self-knowledge owes much to the seventeenth-century 'realist' philosophers La Rochefoucauld, Pascal and La Bruyère, who interpreted human nature largely in terms of vanity, e.g:.

'No matter how well we be spoken of, we are taught nothing thereby we did not already know.' (La Rochefoucauld)

'Curiosity is only vanity. We usually only want to know something so that we can talk about it.' (Pascal)

'Modesty is to merit as shadows are to the figure in a painting: it strengthens it and sets it off.' (La Bruyère)

These maxims and their permutations turn up again and again in Restoration comedies, Silver Fork novels and the literary productions of the 1890s, both in original form and paraphrased. Camp people take a sardonic delight in reducing all motives to vanity, and few things afford them more pleasure than the idea of self-important members of the establishment unwittingly revealing that vanity is the mainspring of all their actions. A classic case is our eavesdropping on Lady Wishfort as she prepares to meet her intended lover, Sir Roland, in William Congreve's *The Way of the World*:

Lady Wishfort: And—well—and how do I look, Foible?
Foible (her maid): Most killing well, madam.
Lady Wishfort: Well, and how shall I receive him? In what figure shall I give his heart the first impression? There is a great deal in the first impression. Shall I sit?—No, I won't sit—I'll walk away—ay, I'll walk from the door upon his entrance and then turn full upon him—No, that will be too

'She is the anti-dote to desire.'
Mrs Pitt as Lady Wishfort in William Congreve's *The Way of the World*, Covent Garden, 1776.

sudden. I'll lie—ay, I'll lie down—I'll receive him in my little dressing-room, there's a couch—yes, yes, I'll give the first impression on a couch—I won't lie neither, but loll and lean upon one elbow; with one foot a little dangling off, jogging in a thoughtful way—yes, O, nothing is more alluring than a levée from a couch in some confusion—it shews the foot to advantage, and furnishes with blushes, and re-composing airs beyond comparison.'

Camp people take a dim view of human nature, one unillumined by notions of sympathy or altruism. We all use our own self-esteem as the measure of others' worth and take our self-love as the pattern for our love of others. Camp people love others as they love themselves, that is to say, not much. They make no allowances, dissecting others' motives in the dispassionate manner of those whose own passions have not been properly reciprocated.

The camp are locked in a tinny world-view in which everyone glitters and rattles—a world that is superficial, brittle and ultimately worthless. This is the brutal cynicism of the adolescent (brutal above all to the person who believes it), but camp people remain trapped in it as long as they evade maturity. 'I wish I hadn't this fatal knack of seeing through people,' complains Florence in *The Vortex* by Noel Coward. This state of affairs, however, does not tip them into tortuous soul-searching. Such introspection would not be camp—a bold face is needed. 'The dandy may be blasé or he may suffer,' said Baudelaire, 'but in the latter case he suffers like the Spartan gnawed by the fox.' And Thomas Lister summarised all camp people when he described his dandy hero, Trebeck, as having 'a heartlessness in his character, a spirit of gay misanthropy'.

There are two main ways in which camp misanthropy expresses itself: through the misogyny inherent in effeminacy and through camp bitchiness. Psychologists claim that effeminate men often nurture feelings of hostility, envy and revenge towards the women they mimic. Not daring to attack directly, they are surreptitiously spiteful. They secretly despise women (and feminists have been quick to pick up on these intimations of contempt). The effeminate man is a caricature of the traditionally feminine woman, belittling her and exaggerating the artificial elements in

The young Cecil Beaton on his carousel bed at Ashcombe; artist Rex Whistler and stage designer Oliver Messel helped to redesign and decorate the house.

her personality to the extent that they become ludicrous. The purely nominal nature of some traditionally feminine gentleness is shown up: the effeminate man is openly bitchy. The teeth and the nails waiting to ambush from somewhere within the softness of the Eternal Feminine are mutated in camp into fangs and claws that can no longer remain hidden.

One qualification: it would be easy to overemphasise camp's misogyny, which in most cases is tempered by a great affection for women. Imitation is a form of flattery even if, as in this case, it can't be said to be particularly sincere. Effeminate men reinforce sexual stereotypes as much as they attack them; they celebrate them as much as they satirise them. The camp love of femininity is often expressed in terms of fanatical admiration of female entertainers. Ronald Firbank, for example, idolised famous actresses of his day, as did Cecil Beaton in his younger, camper days. Camp adoration of Marlene Dietrich and Judy Garland is well known, and the full force of the camp love of unashamed, over-the-top femininity can be seen today at any Shirley Bassey or Diana Ross concert.

Bitchiness, the other element of camp misanthropy is, according to feminists, typical of marginal groups. Elizabeth Janeway writes that women and homosexuals, when excluded from the camaraderie of the man's world, 'develop profoundly ambiguous feelings about any sort of community they may set up for themselves'; they are 'notorious for tight but short-lived cliques and bitter personal rivalries... Cattiness and disloyalty are expected and found among all those who regard part of themselves as unacceptable.' On the other hand, camp bitchiness is a vice dressed up to best advantage. Camp literature is enlivened by a succession of brilliantly bitchy confrontations, such as this from Wilde's *The Importance of Being Earnest*:

Cecily: It would distress me more than I can tell you, dear Gwendolen, if it caused you any mental or physical anguish, but I feel bound to point out that since Earnest proposed to you he clearly has changed his mind.
Gwendolen (meditatively): If the poor fellow has been entrapped into any foolish promise I shall consider it my duty to rescue him at once, and with a firm hand.
Cecily (thoughtfully and sadly): Whatever unfortunate entanglement my dear boy may have got into, I will never reproach him with it after we are married.

Another outstanding feature of the camp performance is its profession of sexual satiety: the languor of the camp manner, its lubricity of voice and perpetually post-coital air, publicises not only boredom, but also sleaziness. The camp person typically presents himself as a sexual Pococurante who has tried everything and subsequently tired of it. The polymorphous perversity which Freud says is in us all, seems to be somehow nearer the surface in the camp.

Shirley Bassey.

99

The literature and art of camp bristle with sexual references: homosexuality in Wilde's *The Picture of Dorian Gray*, lesbianism in Firbank's *The Flower Beneath the Foot*, masochism in Swinburne's *The Flogging Block*, sadism in Gore Vidal's *Myra Breckinridge*, narcissism in the Abbé de Choisy's *Marquise/Marquis de Banneville*, exhibitionism in Frederick Rolfe's *Hadrian VII*. All of these elements seem to be present in Beardsley's drawings, so prominently, in fact, that again one begins to suspect that perhaps he protests too much. Huysmans's dictum comes to mind, 'Only the celibate can be truly obscene,' and close behind it, Wilde's advice never to be discovered on a couch with Aubrey, 'because it's not in the slightest bit compromising.' Beardsley seems to have been a case of extreme desires weakly felt.

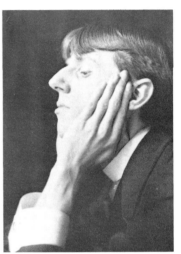

Above: Aubrey Beardsley (1872-98), photographed by F. H. Evans in 1895.
Left: Beardsley's design for the Frontispiece of *Earl Lavender*.

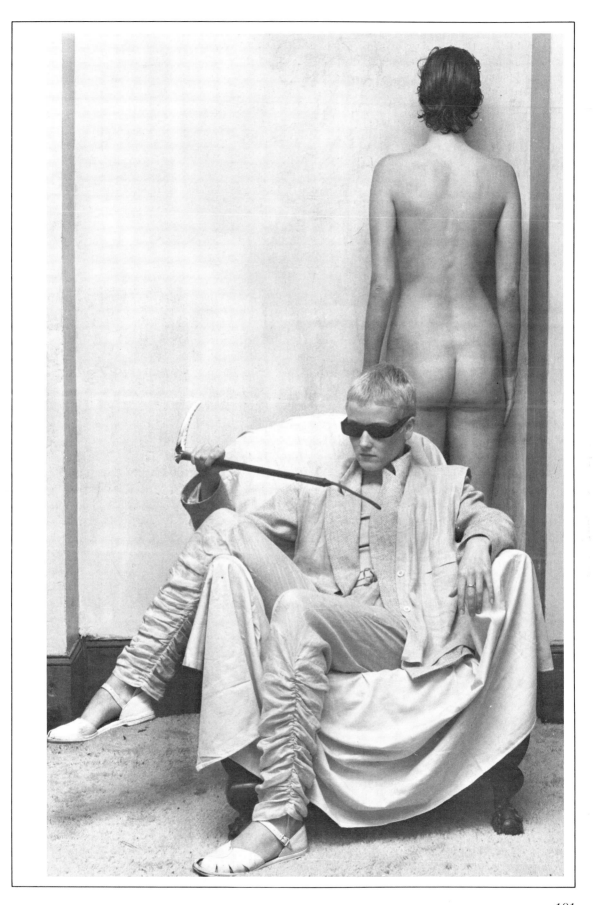

Beardsley's contemporary, Swinburne, who undoubtedly had elements of camp in his make-up, was similarly eccentric. His friend, Dante Gabriel Rossetti, thought it preposterous that England's premier erotic poet should be so innocent. He arranged that Swinburne should spend the night with a circus acrobat, who was paid for her services. In the morning, she had to confess her failure and return Rossetti's money, 'I can't get Mr Swinburne to understand,' she said, 'that biting is not enough.'

Further back in the nineteenth century, Plumer Ward's hero Tremaine was said to be too delicate for amours—he was only up to amourettes. His first whole affair was put an end to in a moment, 'by the unhappy accident of a windy walk up Headington hill. It was not that the fair one's leg was either thick or crooked: for it was even remarkably well shaped. But the scandal went on to say, that a garter which happened to fall on the occasion, was considerably the worse for wear... Another growing passion was reported to have been nipt in the bud by the fair one not being sufficiently sentimental, a third, by her being too much so; a fourth by his detecting her in reading Tom Jones, a fifth by her having eaten her peas with a knife: and scandal added that one of his predilections for a young lady of the very first quality in France, was sickened to death by her telling him one day *qu'elle avait pris médecine*!'

The camp view of desire sees it as a species of disgust: a stirring in the loins is a stern call to duty; humiliation and degradation are in the offing; lust loosens self-control and obscures self-knowledge.

Anthony Storr has attacked the fashionable belief that sexual deviations are glamorous refinements of the sexual instinct, that they are marks of sophistication, the result of breadth of experience and consequent satiety. Sexual deviation, he argues, is the result not of a superabundance of desire, but of a lack of it. Because of some fundamental feeling of inadequacy, the deviate shrinks disgustedly from normal desire and comforts himself with some of its more marginal forms: deviates are all more or less asexual. Camp people might have been made to prove these theories.

The story of camp is that of the Emperor's New Clothes in reverse: the Emperor is clothed, but the crowd is gulled into declaring him indecent. It seems that often the more bizarre and eventful the sexual display, the more uneventful is the sex life behind it. The camp person's sex life has been transferred from the private to the public sphere.

While there are suggestions of most perversions in camp culture, the paradigmatic perversion is exhibitionism. The thing is not to be homosexual, masochistic or whatever, but to be seen to be so. The satisfaction in this display derives, in Havelock Ellis's terms, from the feeling of having effected a 'psychic defloration'. Sexually shocking

Algernon Swinburne—a drawing by Carlo Pellegrini, 1874.

behaviour is of course, natural in the adolescent, expressing the wish to be thought grown-up, but if it persists past adolescence it is likely to create a specifically camp aura.

Camp is shot through with the shocking from the extreme viciousness of the underworld characters described by Jean Genet, from the excesses of the films of Kenneth Anger and Andy Warhol, through the outrageousness of Wilde and the innuendo of Firbank, to the flippancy of Noel Coward and the good-natured burlesque of Danny La Rue. We can find a trace of 'psychic defloration' in Gérard de Nerval's habit of walking in the Bois de Boulogne with a lobster on a leash and in William Beckford's mania for tower building. Nothing that is properly called camp entirely escapes a suspicion of the sexuality of shock.

Another interesting illustration of this phenomenon is to be found in some of the spy films of the early and middle 'sixties. In 1966, Ronald Bryden wrote an article in *The Observer* called '*The Spies Who Came Into Camp*' in which he argued that the comic strip style of such films as *Modesty Blaise* and *Casino Royale* (the 'jump-cut from wish to fulfilment') enables perverse desires to be enjoyed in the socially acceptable guise of parody. 'Within the generalised campness of the spy-spoof films lurks...perversity in masquerade "tailored for" the sexually timid.' He goes on to argue that this stylistic device filtered through to films from the novels of Genet.

Just as one is more likely to have Freudian dreams after reading the works of Freud, these films demonstrate how his theories can be self-fulfilling prophecies. *Modesty Blaise* and the others were clearly made by people who were at least acquainted with Freud's ideas, and plead for a Freudian interpretation along the lines of Ronald Bryden's. Freud's hydraulic model of sexuality, whereby dammed (i.e. socially unacceptable) libido finds a more roundabout route to fulfilment, has become so deeply-seated in our way of thinking as to be almost unquestionable. This model is not helpful, however, in considering the campness of these films, as is apparent if we take up the proferred comparison with the novels of Genet. There, sexual fantasies are thrown into relief by the sordidness of the fantasist's surroundings—a tin of vaseline, a porcelain angel, shady dance halls, false eyelashes, denim. Sex is actual rather than fantasised, and details of the surroundings are mixed in to make the account come alive with a jarring realism. In the film of *Modesty Blaise*, we encounter something quite different. The jump-cut is not, as in Genet, from wish to fulfilment, but from wish to a time after fulfilment has taken place. It does not deal in real desire at all. The perversity of *Modesty Blaise* is only token perversity. Its campness masks not bestial passions (which the Freudian model would lead us to expect) but the lack of them.

The Depths of the Sea by Edward Burne-Jones, whose quivering, dissolving figures have long appealed to camp's elusive sexuality.

'Methinks, a million fools in choir
Are raving and will never tire.'
An illustration by Harry Clarke to

Goethe's *Faust*, translated by John
Anster and published by Harrap
(1925).

Bernard Shaw advanced the view that all superior women are masculine and all superior men are feminine. Certainly the villains in some spoof spy films of the 1960s were sexually ambiguous. *Above:* Lotte Lenya as Colonel Klebb, a Russian agent in the James Bond film, *From Russia With Love* (1963). *Right:* Dirk Bogarde as the villain in Joseph Losey's film *Modesty Blaise* (1966). On the point of dying of thirst in the desert, he is heard to murmur: 'Champagne! Champagne!'.

In comparison with the non-camp novels of Genet, it is escapist in the sense of escaping from the realities of life—work, material want and, above all, sex. Camp wants to escape from rather than to sex.

Pure fantasy is not camp—camp people are tied to reality by their desire for admiration; they always play to an audience, whether literal or figurative, real or imaginary. All their day-dreams are bounded by a proscenium arch or the walls of a drawing room or bar. They dream of grand entrances made, epigrams coined and dresses that kill. Camp people are mythomaniacs, indefatigable self-mythologisers, decking out their personalities with lurid adolescent imaginings.

Perhaps the most transparent example of camp wish-fulfilment in literature is Frederick Rolfe's *Hadrian VII* in which Hadrian daydreams about becoming Pope. What makes this camp escapism is its emphasis on personal adornment and on that side of Roman Catholicism summed up by Sydney Smith as 'Posture and Imposture, flections and genuflections, bowing to the right, curtseying to the left, and an immense amount of man-millinery...'

' "Now perhaps Mrs Strong would like to see the garden," he presently said. It was a very happy thought. His Holiness carried His little yellow cat, and they all went down together; and strolled about the woods and the box-alleys and the vineyards. They picked the flowers; and the children picked the fruit. They admired the peacocks: and rested on white marble hemicycles in the sun-flecked shade of cypresses; and they talked of this, that, and the other, as well as these and those. A chamberlain came through the trees, and delivered a small veiled salver to the gentleman who followed the pontifical party at fifty paces. At the moment of departure he came near. The salver contained five little crosses of gold and chrysoberyls set in diamonds. Three were elaborate and two severely plain. Hadrian presented them to His guests.   "You will accept a memorial of this happy day; and of course" (with that rare dear smile of his) "you will not expect the Pope to give you anything but popery. Good-bye, dear friends, good-bye.'

A Fairy Prince by Charles Conder: camp day-dreams of sumptuous self-display.

Ecclesiastical contexts have given camp opportunities for irreverence, whether in the novels of Ronald Firbank and Frederick Rolfe or in the poetry of Ronald Knox and John Betjeman; the references are used rather differently in the photography of Jean-Marc Prouveur.

"How He has improved!" said the dark girl, as they went out.

"O mother, and did you see the buckles on His shoes!" said the fair one.

"I call Him a topper," said the boy.'

Rolfe makes much of the cross-sexual connotations of clerical garb, but nothing comes of them. The threat of real sex is embodied by Hadrian's sweaty ex-landlady, Mrs Crowe, who follows him to Rome and seeks, by threats of blackmail, to bend him to her rapacious will.

The falseness of camp's claims to be vain and to be satiated are connected to the duplicity that has been seen as an integral part of the homosexual's unhappy lot. In order to live a life free from persecution, the true homosexual may find himself concealing his sexual nature and thus, in a sense, betray his fellow homosexuals. On the other hand, when he is with his own kind, he is false to his public image and so, in a sense, betraying the people with whom he is in daily contact, at the factory, office or whatever.

At this point, it is worth looking again at the relationship between camp and homosexuality, which undeniably exists, but is not the simple equation that it is often supposed to be.

In a fascinating passage in his autobiographical *Thief's Journal*, Jean Genet describes how he felt the need in adolescence to become what he had been accused of being (i.e. 'a fairy'), to play up to the prejudices that the community had formed against him. In other words, if he were going to be thought objectionable, he might as well act in such a way as to deserve it.

Jean Cocteau's *L'Espionne* (The Spy): the exhilarations of deceit.

The analogy with the feminist analysis of feminine suggests that homosexuals, having discovered their sexual nature, are pressured into adopting the camp mode of behaviour that society deems appropriate for them.

If Genet's observation is accurate, this analogy, in some cases at least, puts the cart before the horse. It would be truer to say that people who have discovered in themselves a taste for camp behaviour are pressured into allowing themselves to be thought homosexual, since in society's simplistic view, these two characteristics are to be equated. The idea of homosexuality then, is a rationalisation of a more generalised feeling of exclusion and marginality. Unsure of himself, an individual embraces this idea of homosexuality and the hostility it attracts. Fear and aggression feed off one another, so that the camp person, by defensively anticipating prejudices, creates them.

The idea that there is a necessary connection between homosexuality and camp is a relatively recent one. There was never any suggestion of Boni de Castellane being homosexual. For all their effeminacy, Disraeli and Bulwer Lytton were never thought so. The fops of Restoration comedies were above all ladies' men, their effeminacy being an expression of their (usually thwarted) wish to ingratiate themselves with women; such a motive is also to be discerned in the camp behaviour of two fops in the following literary curio of 1580, an extract from a novella by Francesco Sansovino (son of Jacopo Sansovino, architect of the Library of St Mark in Venice):

'During fine summer weather they were in the habit of wearing the most costly white silk dresses, their vests were of white velvet, their ruffs of the whitest cambric, their pantaloons and stockings of white silk, and their hats of white velvet with white feathers in them. And yet they had the assurance to appear thus accoutred in public, displaying their feathers with all the vanity of peacocks, as they turned arm in arm along the piazzas, full of their own perfections and eager to attract the notice of spectators who failed not indeed to smile as they passed; they frequented the neighbourhood…in order to make themselves agreeable to a party of ladies.'

Recently, attention has been focused on the connection between homosexuality and duplicity by the various spy scandals. Secret work, it has been suggested, appeals to some element in the homosexual nature; justifying betrayal for ideological reasons, ideology soon becomes merely a pretext for betrayal. Genet has written about the experience of being a spy:

John Osborne's *A Patriot For Me*, first performed in a club production outside the Lord Chamberlain's jurisdiction in 1965. The play tells the story of the spy, Colonel Redl, played here by Maximilian Schell.

'Perhaps I also wanted to alienate myself further from my own country. In any event, I mean that as a result of a certain frame of mind which is natural to enchantment... I was ready to act not in accordance with the rules of morality but in accordance with certain laws of a fictional aesthetic which makes the spy out to be a restless, invisible, though powerful character.'

Camp people enjoy the idea that others are never sure of what they are thinking, that they are holding back secret knowledge. This is perhaps related to the pleasure that a transvestite feels when he fools others into thinking him a woman, described here by Ronald Firbank in *The Eccentricities of Cardinal Pirelli*:

'The dear street... The quickening stimulus of the crowd: truly it was exhilarating to mingle freely with the throng!

'Disguised as...a matron, (disliking to forgo altogether the militant bravoura of a skirt), it became possible to combine philosophy, equally, with pleasure...

'Purring to himself, and frequently pausing, he made his way, by ecstatic degrees, towards the mirador on the garden wall.

'Although a mortification, it was imperative to bear in mind the consequences of cutting a too dashing figure. Beware display. Vanity once had proved all but fatal: "I remember it was the night I wore ringlets and was called 'my queen' ".'

With their quick and ready appreciation of the undercurrents of vanity in any behaviour, the camp rejoice in being one step ahead of everyone else. It might, for example, be objected that the idea of the spy as an invisible, powerful character is purely fictional; the camp person would already be fully aware of this and would have worked out all its ironic implications—criticism by outsiders is otiose. In an article in *The Times*, Leo Abse argued a forceful case for the connection between homosexuality and betrayal:

'From James I, of whom it was said he gave his money to his favourites and state secrets to everyone, down to Blunt, treachery is uncomfortably linked with disturbed homosexuals unable to come to terms with their sexual destiny. That is a harsh judgement, but consider some of our homosexual traitors and spies. Blunt, Burgess, Maclean and Vassall are but the end of a long line stretching from Lord Henry Howard, Francis Bacon, Christopher Marlowe and Antonio Perez. In this century, two of the most notorious traitors, the Austrian Colonel Redl and the tragic Roger Casement, were compulsive and bizarre homosexuals.'

Disturbed homosexuals, Abse infers, should not be entrusted with state secrets; history shows, he argues, that there is a connection between abnormality and compulsive disloyalty. With the sort of screening that Mr Abse suggests, Burgess, Vassall and Blunt would not have been recruited for the secret service. The warning signs were there for all to see.

Before the war, Burgess was a great friend of Brian Howard, and they went raging round Soho and the back streets of Salzburg together. The two men had much in common. Both were garrulous megalomaniacs who experimented with Wildean poses. Each had at some time been called the most brilliant man of his generation.

In *A Chapter of Accidents*, Goronwy Rees describes Burgess's flat at this time. It was decorated in red, white and blue, which Burgess said was the only colour scheme any reasonable man could find supportable. A model of a Royal Navy frigate in a glass bottle was prominently displayed. Scattered untidily aound the room were his favourite books—*Middlemarch*, *Martin Chuzzlewit* and Lady Gwendolen Cecil's biography of Lord Salisbury. It is clear from *A Chapter of Accidents* that, in a way, Burgess loved England and everything typically English. He was committed to it, but not in a way that was serious enough to preclude his betrayal of it. In retrospect, it is apparent that he saw England in decline as having become something marginal. Perhaps Burgess's purely decorative use of the colours of the Union Jack and his fad for Victoriana were an anticipation of the military uniform/Lord Kitchener style that was to become popular in the 1960s. At any rate, Guy Burgess's camp attitude to the British Empire played a small but significant part in its downfall.

In *The Climate of Treason*, Andrew Boyle records that Burgess explained his disturbed patterns of behaviour in terms of a traumatic childhood experience. He was awakened during the night by a scream from his parents' bedroom. Bursting in, he found his mother struggling helpplessly underneath the lifeless body of his father, who, it transpired, had died during the act of making love. We should not let ourselves be too horrified by this anecdote, though. There is a very good chance that it is simply not true. As became obvious from his appetite for espionage, there were few things that Guy Burgess enjoyed more than lying.

The talent for lying, for making a virtue out of duplicity, is a mark of camp. Freed from the tyranny of integrity, having thrown off the shackles of sincerity, the camp person is elated to discover within himself seemingly limitless possibilities for self-projection. He is suffused with a spirit of playfulness, free to toy with as many different roles as he likes, and to attitudinise amusingly.

The camp mind has no causal nexus, no unifying principle. Such opposites as cynicism and sentimentality, envy and affection, indecency and fastidiousness, individuality and imitation, are not attracted to one another in it, but

Part of the 1981 annual International Lesbian/Gay Freedom Day Parade in San Francisco.

remain suspended in constant, uneasy opposition. They do not, as in more conventional minds, modify one another. Their stark juxtapositions are reflected throughout all aspects of camp culture. We find it in Burgess's political duplicity, in Warhol's commitment to trash and in the sardonic enjoyment of sentimental songs which is such a common feature of camp behaviour.

The camp are unabashedly insincere, and go out of their way to advertise this to others. They can thus forestall any aggression that their outrageousness might provoke. This involves making playful and placatory gestures of submission—'Don't hit me, I didn't mean it',—representing the camp person as too marginal to be taken seriously, so not worth hating. The stock gestures of camp elicit no more than stock gestures of hostility: danger is defused.

Camp's wilful insincerity shows contempt for contempt, the wider implication being that ethical values are not worth taking seriously.

Genet has developed this idea at some length. It first appears in the novel, *Our Lady of the Flowers*. The transvestite, Divine, is sitting in a queens' bar, wearing a little coronet of fake pearls. When she bursts out laughing, the coronet falls to the floor, scattering. Contempt threatens to engulf Divine, but she transcends it by her bravura. Plucking her false teeth from her mouth, she sets them in

Opposite: The Cycle Sluts.

the coronet's place. 'Dammit all, Ladies, I'll be queen anyhow!'

Similarly, in *The Thief's Journal*, Genet describes a ceremony held by the Carolinas, a group of transvestites who wore shawls, mantillas and silk dresses, to mourn the destruction of a favourite *pissoir*. Walking in procession, carrying a wreath of red roses to lay in commemoration at the site, they managed 'to carry the thing off with a kind of wild extravagance.' Laughter could not hurt them. They managed, it seemed to Genet, to 'pierce the shell of the world's contempt.'

Perhaps it was this idea in particular which attracted Sartre to the work of Genet. Just as Sartre's philosophy talks, at one stage, of going through the other side of despair, Genet's, which is a show-off's counterpart of the same, teaches going through to the other side of shame. It is an idea that recalls one of Aretino's letters, which contrasts Honour with Shame, the latter living in utter freedom, playing stupendous jokes on the former, tripping him up as he walks ponderously by. Diderot, too, talked of outrages of such enormity that they put their perpetrators beyond the reach of mere contempt; and in *Venus and Tannhäuser*, Beardsley suggests that the very excess and violence of a fault may be its excuse.

From the different strands of camp psychology—the protestations of vanity and satiety, the psychic deflorations, the candid insincerity and the disconcerting contempt for contempt—a pattern emerges: they are all traits which spring from a wish to make a startling impact, to make a splash. The desire to shine is a very human one and a very natural one, though. In what circumstances does it become camp, as it is, say, in *Pelham*:

'On entering Paris, I had resolved to set up "a character" for I was always of an ambitious nature and desirous of being distinguished from the ordinary herd. After various cogitations as to the particular one I should assume, I thought nothing appeared more likely to be obnoxious to men, and therefore pleasing to women, than an egregious coxcomb: accordingly I arranged my hair into ringlets...'

Although camp is an extreme form of other-directed behaviour, its many-layered ironies contrast with the straightforward nature of healthy extroversion. The secure sense of selfhood and confidence about the place of self in the world that are the mainsprings of normal extrovert behaviour are hardly to be found in camp. Its mentality is too complex: camp people want to be centre of attention but do not naturally overflow with high spirits; they are not usually the life and soul of the party.

'Shyness,' said Hugh Kingsmill, 'is egoism out of its depth.' One might go on from there to say that camp is egoism out of its depth and furiously waving. It is a desperate measure for overcoming shyness. It is a fancy dress of the personality that lends boldness to timidity and propels the backward forward. In effect, it is a sham extroversion.

This is why camp people often have an air of embarrassed boldness, why it sometimes seems that they have too much self-confidence and sometimes too little. Even in Robert de Montesquiou, from whom one might have expected complete social mastery, camp's internal conflict was very obvious. According to Alphonse Daudet, his conversation consisted of long monologues, which were slangy, erudite and full of innuendo, but would lurch to a finish, at which point he would screech with effeminate and almost hysterical laughter, and then try to control himself by slapping his hand over his mouth.

In R.D. Laing's *The Divided Self*, there is a description of a self-conscious exhibitionist in whom many of these camp traits are clearly recognisable. 'He is driven compulsively to seek company but never allows himself to be himself in the presence of others...he plays an elaborate game of pretence and equivocation... He appears to be extremely narcissistic and exhibitionistic...he compulsively exhibits what he regards as mere extraneous trappings to others; he dresses ostentatiously, speaks loudly and insistently. He is constantly drawing attention to himself and at the same time drawing attention *away* from himself.'

Psychologists have not dealt with camp behaviour by name, but analogy with analyses by Freud, Ellis, Storr, Laing and Stoller, of closely related, if not identical, behaviour confirms that camp people's dealings with others are characterised by showing-off, secrecy, misanthropy and sentimentality, all of which skirt round the mature, fulfilled relationship that ideally dominates the non-camp person's mental make-up. Camp comforts itself not only with the more marginal forms of sexuality, but also with the more marginal forms of emotional fulfilment which are their counterparts.

This psychological view of camp needs to be put in perspective. It is significant that Laing talks about his subject acting 'compulsively'. As a scientist, Laing is concerned to show that people run smoothly according to established laws. Any deviation from the norm is seen in terms of symptoms, an approach that unavoidably diminishes the importance of free choice, even though Laing himself is actively concerned to emphasise its importance. Inevitably, psychology's starting point is a form of determinism.

To talk of camp in terms of compulsions or people being driven is to prejudge the issue of whether anyone might reasonably choose to adopt a camp style of living, of whether, in fact, camp might have a valid ideological dimension.

A psychological analysis tends, by its very nature, to have a levelling effect. It carries with it the implication that we should all be less like Pelham and more like Mr Pooter.

But apologists for camp would see it as missing the point to discuss camp pleasures as merely compensatory, camp represents an attempt to make such supposed compensations more desirable than the things they are nominally compensating for. It may be a conscious attempt made with some courage. 'Remember,' said Pelham, 'that none but those whose courage is unquestionable can venture to be effeminate.' It was a sentiment developed by Robert de Montesquiou in a poem:

The effeminate fights, the effeminate avenges itself,
The effeminate conquers.
The effeminate works and thinks and over the morass
Of opaque and heavy male predominates and exults.
In himself, the effeminate contains more than one race,
    Yes, more than one sex also,
He is indefatigable when others are exhausted,
And deceit and anxiety only lend him strength.

In this examination of the history and psychology of camp, one idea has reappeared again and again in different guises: the idea of making the best of a bad job, of turning disadvantages into advantages. It seems, ironically enough, that camp is a form of pragmatism. Arising from a failure to cope with the relativity of social roles, camp strives to make a virtue of that failure. Insincerity is an ineradicable part of human nature, says camp, so one is going against the grain in trying to eradicate it; instead one should try to exploit its humorous and life-enhancing possibilities. This idea is dramatised in the novels of Carl Van Vechten. In *The Blind Bow Boy*, for example, the innocent Harold Prewett is introduced by his father to the sophisticated camp circles which revolve around Campaspe Lorillard and the Duke of Middlebottom. When, at the end of the book, he discovers that his father's secret intention has been to turn him against their trivial, elegant life-style, he embraces it, even though it had been becoming repellent to him; the moral is that it is better to associate with people like Campaspe and Middlebottom, who are openly duplicitous, than with Harold's industrialist father, who is furtively so. Similarly, in *The Tattooed Countess*, the countess herself, who wears a tattoo on her arm as a token of affection from her last lover, is contrasted favourably with the prurient, small-minded hypocrites who spend their days gossiping about her. Better to live a life of overt pleasure than one of sour and envious respectability. 'We try harder to appear happy than we do to be happy.' (La Rochefoucauld.) In camp philosophy, this view of the absurdity of human nature acquires the force of a guiding principle: in order to be happy, concentrate your efforts on appearing so. The greatest happiness is to be found in the eyes of others. Since we must be vain, let us play it to the hilt.

Camp Insights

Literary forms: salon verse, drawing-room books and albums, poetry, comedies, novels. Archetypes: Dandy Wit, Phallic Woman, Eminence Cerise, Transvestite, Burlesque Woman, Bourgeois Gentilhomme, Manic Poseur, Vamp. Styles: exoticism, revivalism, nostalgie de la boue. Good/Bad and So-Bad-It's-Good. The Trash Aesthetic. Andy Warhol versus the Abstract Expressionists. Pop music rescued from pomposity: Glam Rock, Punk, Disco, New Romantics.

Vincent Voiture (1598-1648).

Camp literature fans out from the epigram. Inconsistent and amusing, the epigram is the expression of the camp view of life, embodying both delight in the devious and dislike of the difficult. At its best, the epigram adds extreme artificiality to an air of spontaneity; it has been born in response to the inspiration of the moment, but at the end of a long and distinguished line of witticisms; glittering balefully, it springs fully-formed from the camp wit's head. Above all, it is designed to display its author as dextrous, urbane and lighthearted.

An improvisational air carries over into salon verses, some of the better of which are camp. The person who more or less originated salon verse was the *précieux* poet, Vincent Voiture. His innovations in seventeenth-century verse forms set the style, and subsequent salon verse followed his example in its jaunty rhythms, its emphatic and sometimes witty rhymes, it cliquishness (with recondite allusions to members of the poet's own salon) and its occasional scurrility; this riddle by Voiture is a masterpiece of innuendo:

> *De quelque éclat que je puisse briller,*
> *Souvent le plus galant pâlit à me voir nue,*
> *Alexandre se plut à me déshabiller,*
> *Darius eût voulu ne m'avoir jamais vue.*

Salon verses underwent a great revival in Regency England, when the drawing-room books and albums of the day provided an arena for ready wit and facetious ingenuity. The specially designed drawing room books (as distinct from such books as *The Corsair* and *Vivian Grey*, which came to be used as conversation pieces in drawing rooms) were highly decorative annuals, usually edited by ladies of fashion, who persuaded celebrities to contribute little verses and other literary trifles. (The attempt to combine fashion with literature is typically camp.) One of the more popular of these books was *The Keepsake*: the title page of its 1829 edition contains a typically fey engraving of 'Fancy descending among the muses'. Charles Greville called drawing-room books those 'gorgeous inanities' containing 'poetical effusions of the smallest possible merit, but exciting interest and curiosity from the notoriety of their authors,' and in *Diary of a Désennuyée*, Mrs Gore disparagingly refers to the 'embroidered-cambric-handkerchief' school of literature. Apart from these printed books, there were the albums, again highly decorative, usually owned by young ladies who cajoled the famous (or just their cleverer friends) into contributing funny or sentimental bits of poetry or prose. Literary standards in these albums were even lower than in the drawing-room books. This fact together with the preponderant sentimentality naturally piqued the interest and wit of people of camp sensibility: Bulwer Lytton told a friend that a blue-stocking had asked him to write in her album:

'Teased into compliance, I wrote:
"Fools write here to show their wit
And men of sense to laugh at it."
I need not tell you that the Blue looked exceedingly black.'

The best known album was kept by Beau Brummell. His was a thick quarto in vellum, bound in dark blue velvet and embossed in silver gilt. It included frilly little verses like 'The Contents of a Lady's Toilet Table Drawer', which was contributed by a lady who visited him in exile in Caen.

Perhaps uniquely in modern popular song, Noel Coward has caught the mixture of stylishness and gaiety, the unusual rhythms and the breath-taking rhymes that characterise camp *vers de société*. The elaborate euphemisms of 'Mrs Worthington' suddenly erupt into crudity; 'I've been to a marvellous party' and 'Nina' have double and sometimes triple rhymes ('candour' with 'Carmen Miranda' with 'propaganda', and 'behaviour' with 'Belgravia'); and there is an outrageous Coward version of Cole Porter's 'Let's do it, let's fall in love':

> He said that Belgians and Greeks do it,
> Nice young men who sell antiques do it,
> Let's do it, let's fall in love.
> Monkeys whenever you look do it,
> Aly Khan and King Farouk do it,
> Let's do it, let's fall in love.
> Louella Parsons can't-quite-do-it
> Because she's so highly strung,
> Marlene—might do it
> But she looks much too young...

Of the camp poetry that is too considered and finely wrought to be called society verse, the most outstanding and influential example is Alexander Pope's *The Rape of the Lock*, which shows a camp commitment to trivia by its mock-heroic treatment of a petty squabble. Its elaborate form is out of proportion to its slight subject matter, which, like all camp literature, might feature in the gossip column

Opposite:
'The peer now spreads the glittering forfex wide,
To inclose the Lock; now joins it, to divide.'
One of Aubrey Beardsley's illustrations to *The Rape of the Lock*.

of a society journal. Epigram, invocation, simile and anti-thesis call attention to themselves in order to highlight the writer's own virtuosity, (the 'art that conceals art' has no place here), to promote the idea of cleverness in general and to help induce the ironic distancing of mind that is an essential part of camp. The tone is charming. It flatters the reader by being arch and conspiratorial, addressing him, often directly, in mock-aristocratic style as a fellow member of the aristocracy. The rules of polite society apply (though of a polite society that may never have existed except in camp's bogus but nonetheless delightful fancies). Strong emotions are not expressed or referred to, except in terms of humorous understatement or hyperbole, which seek to make light of them and so to avoid the imputation of impropriety. The author's presence is scrupulously polite (even to the point of being slightly archaic) but he always has a mischievous twinkle in his eye.

The Rape of the Lock concerns a love-sick baron's stealing of a lock of hair from the beautiful Belinda. Belinda appeals to the gods for its return. They respond by wafting the hair into the sky to form a new constellation, and so declare the apotheosis of a lock of hair. The mock-heroic style has an irreverent attitude to classical deities:

> For this, ere Phoebus rose, he had implored
> Propitious Heaven, and every power adored,
> But chiefly Love—to Love an altar built,
> Of twelve vast French romances, neatly gilt.
> There lay three garters, half a pair of gloves,
> And all the trophies of his former loves;
> With tender billet-doux he lights the pyre,
> And breathes three amorous sighs to raise the fire.

Some of camp's best effects come from variations on this joke. In *Zuleika Dobson*, which translates the style of *The Rape of the Lock* into prose, Max Beerbohm reproves Zeus for not being self-confident enough to appear to his girl-friends in his own person, always having to transform himself into a shape he thinks more likely to be pleasing: as when his Zeus appears to Clio 'flashed down in the semblance of Kinglake's *Invasion of the Crimea*.' Edith Sitwell was also much influenced by *The Rape of the Lock's* mocking attitudes to myths. Her satyr, Scarabombadon, seems camp enough:

> The Satyr Scarabombadon
> Pulled periwig and breeches on
> 'Grown old and stiff, this modern dress
> Adds monstrously to my distress.
> The gout with a hoofen heel
> It's very hard to bear; I feel
> When crushed into a buckled shoe
> The twinge will be redoubled, too.'

The deepest, most meaningful achievements of poetry are

denied to camp, and so are its soaring heights (camp is too crabbed for that), but camp poetry can be delightful: *The Rape of the Lock* and Edith Sitwell's *Façade* are the twin pinnacles of silliness in English literature.

In the theatre, Molière's advances in technique were necessary preconditions for the arrival of camp. *Les Pré-cieuses Ridicules* (1659) has been called the first Comedy of Manners, though in view of such antecedents as *The Knight of the Burning Pestle* (1613) it would perhaps be more accurate to call it the first Comedy of Manners in an elegant setting. Molière's fops were the forerunners of Lord Foppington and Sir Fopling Flutter. The English playwrights of the Restoration had a greater distance, both in space and in irony, from the mannerisms of the aristocracy. Somewhere in that extra distance, camp drama was born—somewhere, moreover, in the margins of Molière's magnificent achievement.

Molière's comedies usually end in the traditional way, with a marriage or batch of marriages, but in Restoration comedies, marriages are at most a cursory genuflection in the direction of morality and often just a mockery of it. George Farquhar's *The Beaux Stratagem* even ends with a batch of divorces. In Molière and earlier comedies, affectations, vanities, misunderstandings and raillery are understood to have been a brief holiday from moral seriousness and to end with marriage. In camp comedies, on the other hand, they are understood to be the facts of life which will remain true, marriage or no marriage. Sir John Vanbrugh's *The Relapse* is a sequel to Colley Cibber's *Love's Last Shift*, in which Loveless, the fop who married at the end of Cibber's play, returns to his old ways. The repentance of the fops at the end of Restoration comedies does not convince: Dormiant and Mirabell will never reform. Their disguises, affectations and so on are represented as in no way regrettable, but rather as aspects of a world that is more amusing, more luxurious and more fun than that outside the theatre. A good production of a Restoration play can make us feel that life might be better if it were more camp.

Recently, some critics have revolted against the traditional interpretation of Restoration comedies and have tried to show that their morality is not significantly different from that of the Sermon on the Mount; audiences may be grateful, though, that they are more amusing. Much of the enjoyment lies in the interplay of amoral, sometimes malicious wit: 'Every page,' writes William Hazlitt, 'presents a shower of brilliant conceits, a tissue of epigrams, a new triumph of wit, a new conquest over dullness. The fire of artful raillery is nowhere else so well kept-up.'

Busy: Ah, the difference that is between you and my Lady Dapper! How uneasy she is if the least thing be amiss about her!

Harriet: She is indeed most exact. Nothing is ever wanting to make her ugliness remarkable...
Busy: I hope, without offence one may endeavour to make oneself agreeable?
Harriet: Not when 'tis impossible. Women then ought to be no more fond of dressing than fools should be of talking. (George Etherege, *The Man of Mode.*)

Generally speaking, the more successful parts of camp novels are those which simply transfer dramatic or comic modes from the stage to the page, for example the scenes of Comedy of Manners in Silver Fork novels, *Zuleika Dobson* and *The Unbearable Bassington*.

'Isn't he at an agricultural college or something of the sort?'
'Yes, studying to be a gentleman farmer, he told me. I didn't ask if both subjects were compulsory.'
'You're really rather dreadful,' said Lady Veula, trying to look as if she thought so; 'remember, we are all equal in the sight of Heaven.'
... If I and Ernest Klopstock are really equal in the sight of Heaven,' said Youghal, with intense complacency, 'I should recommend Heaven to consult an eye specialist.' (Saki, *The Unbearable Bassington.*)

Where such comedy is filled out with other modes, such as philosophical dissertation (*Tremaine*) Byronic adventure (*Pelham*) or Gothic horror and social realism (*The Picture of Dorian Gray*), these elements jostle uneasily with one another.

Because the novel demands a much more sustained effort of creation than the short poem or the comedy, it is more liable to show up weaknesses in the camp aesthetic. Attention to trivial detail is often developed at the expense of overall form—camp novels are seldom very good as novels. Sincerity is to the mind what discipline is to the army, and without it effectiveness is speedily dissipated. Camp writers often lack the energy needed for a full-length novel. They cannot master the broad sweep of the writer wholly confident in his powers. They describe gaiety and fanciful extravagance, but frequently fail to achieve those qualities in their writing: they are light-headed, rather than light-hearted. Camp novels often betray a thinness of ideas which a fitful inventiveness of language does very little to disguise.

In their over-eagerness to shine, camp writers often plagiarise. Disraeli was a voracious, almost indiscriminate plagiarist and an alarming number of the things that Oscar Wilde is famous for having said were not invented by him. In their impatience to impress, camp writers often fill their novels with undigested bits of information, sometimes in long lists of more curiosity value than relevance. These lists are perhaps the literary manifestation of the camp

DON TARQUINIO

A KATALEPTIC PHANTASMATIC
ROMANCE

BY

FR. ROLFE
AUTHOR OF "HADRIAN THE SEVENTH," ETC.

LONDON
CHATTO & WINDUS
1905

Cover and title page of the first edition of *Don Tarquinio*.

mania for collecting. Just as camp people embellish their individuality with collections of unique objects, so camp writers shore up their uniqueness with catalogues.

In Frederick Rolfe's *Don Tarquinio* the 'magic' properties of fetishes to enhance their owner are made explicit:

'But my discourse was so pleasing to Ippolito that, when I had made an end of speaking, he sent to me a page with a tray of rings for mine acceptance. Wherefrom I chose *vj* for the adornment of my thumbs and my first-fingers and my third-fingers: *videlicet* a cockatrice, intagliate in green jasper, for averting the evil eye: a fair boy's head well-combed, intagliate in smaragd, for preserving joy: an Apollino with a necklace of herbs, intagliate in heliotrope, which conferreth invisibility when anointed with marigold-juice…'

Van Vechten's *Peter Whiffle* actually contains a catalogue of catalogues.

Too often, camp writers try too hard for dazzling effects, and succeed only in producing damp squibs:

'Ah, Dorian, how happy you are! What an exquisite life you have had! You have drunk deeply of everything. You have crushed the grapes against your palate.' (Wilde, *The Picture of Dorian Gray*.)

123

The unresolved opposites in the camp mind sometimes result in uncomfortable ambiguities; in *Vathek*, William Beckford clearly did not resolve conflicting desires to write beautifully and humorously, with the result that a description of an idyllic oriental scene will be punctured by an ill-defined joke, creating something that is neither beautiful nor funny. The equivocation of the camp personality does not always transfer well into literature.

There is a certain predictability in camp psychological analysis, a vein that has been mined many times since La Rochefoucauld. Nothing is latent in camp literature; everything is on the surface.

It would be wrong to dwell further on the formal qualities of camp literature. Camp poems, plays and novels are clever trifles, but trifles nonetheless. There is a story about an earnest Siegfried Sassoon going to see Ronald Firbank to ask him about his literary principles. The only response he managed to evince, apart from nervous giggles, was 'My dear, I *adore* italics, don't you?'

Treating Jung's ideas with less respect than they deserve, we can now examine the archetypes of camp—figures who recur in camp literature and culture. This is not to say, of course, that they do not appear in other spheres, but that they do appear in camp more frequently and with more particular connotations.

The Dandy Wit is the idealised self-image of the camp man—urbane, detached, sardonic and poised. Economically secure, he is usually an aristocrat—though an idealised aristocrat, since his mind is obviously too sharp to have been softened by generations of privilege. He represents camp's alternative to conventional maturity: successful in his own terms, which he makes society at large accept, he whips the world into shape with his tongue. In camp circles he is supreme. Lister's hero, Trebeck, is said to be able to 'depress pretensions of a season's standing by the raising of an eyebrow.'

The Dandy Wit is a dilettante, a gifted amateur. One aspect of his seeming knowingness is his conviction that, although in fable the tortoise may beat the hare, in life the hare may stop to take a nap, flip idly through a fashion magazine, pare his nails and still put on a spurt to win.

Models in life and literature include Brummell, Pelham, Trebeck, Disraeli, Wilde, Lord Wotton, the Duke of Dorset, Bassington, Addison de Witt in the film *All About Eve* and Gore Vidal.

Dandy Wits who really are aristocrats are specially prized. Gerald Tyrwhitt-Wilson, Baron Berners, was a Dandy Wit of almost visionary silliness. He is remembered for his barbs, for instance, his complaint about a socially ambitious woman, that he had not been able to sleep in the room next to her because 'she never stopped climbing all night'. More inspired were his pranks, such as installing a

Hurd Hatfield in the striped suit plays the title rôle in Albert Lewin's film of Oscar Wilde's *The Picture of Dorian Gray.*

spinet and a porcelain turtle in his Rolls Royce, or his dyeing a flock of pigeons green, pink, blue and scarlet, or, most startlingly, building a folly, a tower 140 feet high, topped by a huge lantern, and with a notice at the foot of the stairs: 'Members of the public committing suicide from the Tower do so at their own risk.' He was commissioned by Diaghilev to write a ballet, and also wrote many smaller pieces, including a jolly little tune entitled 'Funeral March for a Rich Aunt'. His friend Sir Osbert Sitwell said of him that in his company one felt that anything might happen.

There is perhaps an unconscious poignancy about the ideal of the Dandy Wit, for it shows how, even in his wildest dreams, the camp person is a solitary figure. Lister's Trebeck 'judged that the *éclat* of his character would be somewhat sullied if he were often to expose it to the rude heat of familiar intimacy.' In his uniform the dandy may impress by the sweep of his lapels or by the cut of his trousers, but out of it his splendour may be considerably diminished. Frederick Rolfe's Arthur is similarly aloof:

'The proud gait of the stainless pure secure in himself, wholly perfect in himself, severe with himself as with all, strong in disgust of ill, utterly careless save to keep high,

Dandy wit, Lord Berners, photographed by Cecil Beaton. Beaton records in his diaries that Berners's mother was 'Amusement First'.

Divine, one of the more harrowing incarnations of the Phallic Woman, has starred in *Pink Flamingoes* in which he played The World's Filthiest Person, *Eat Your Make-up*, *Mondo Trasho* and, most recently, *Polyester*.

clean, cold, armed intact, apart, glistening with candid candour both of heart and aspect, like a flower, like a maid, like a star.'

Those who set themselves up on a pedestal are punished: they cannot enjoy the benefits of the admiration they excite.

Complications in camp literature usually spring from a Phallic Woman, a phenomenon which in turn derives from a Freudian concept: that an infant boy may fear that the lack of a penis in his mother implies the possibility of his own castration. A man dressed as a woman, or a woman who is overtly masculine, may lessen the implications of his mother's supposed castration. The

Edith Evans as Lady Bracknell in Anthony Asquith's film of Oscar Wilde's *The Importance of Being Earnest*:
Lady Bracknell: Good afternoon, dear Algernon, I hope you're behaving very well.
Algernon: I'm feeling very well, Aunt Augusta.
Lady Bracknell: That's not quite the same thing. In fact the two things rarely go together.

image of the Phallic Woman is therefore both a grotesque source of anxiety and a strange sort of comfort. Three Phallic Women who terrorise the camp imagination are Caligula and Nero, as described by Suetonius, and Elagabulus, as described by Herodian and Don Cassius. Caligula wore women's clothes, dressed up as Venus and showed his taste for the grotesque by organising comic duels between disabled people. Nero had the boy Sporus castrated and then went through a wedding ceremony with him, dressing himself in a bridal veil. Most notoriously, Elagabulus, who first entered Rome as Emperor wearing a tiara and bracelets adorned with gems, and who painted his eyes and rouged his cheeks, thought it fun to have his boy-friends smothered to death under a deluge of rose petals.

Opposite: The Prince Regent. Camp people often let their vanity get the better of them, and sometimes without offering much resistance.

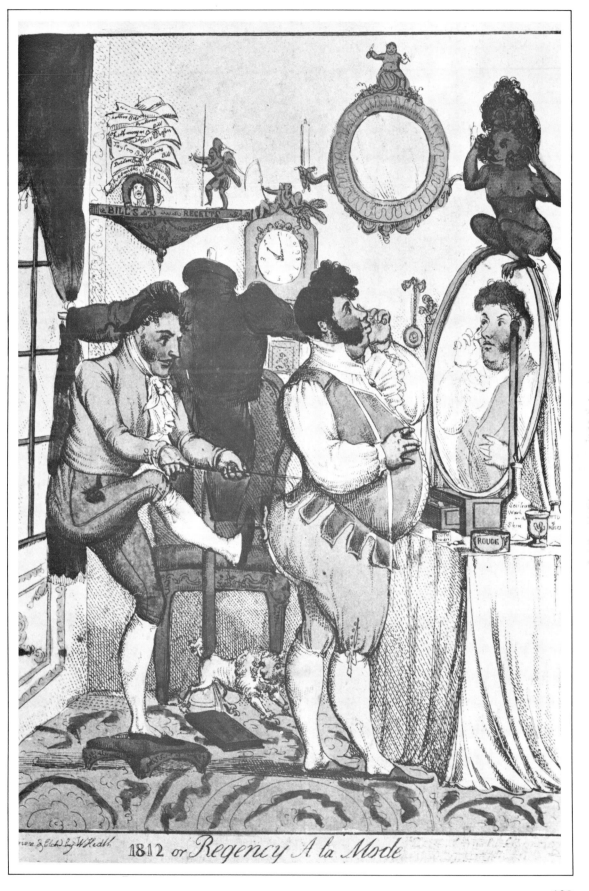

Etchd & Pubd by W. Heath 1812 or *Regency A la Mode*

129

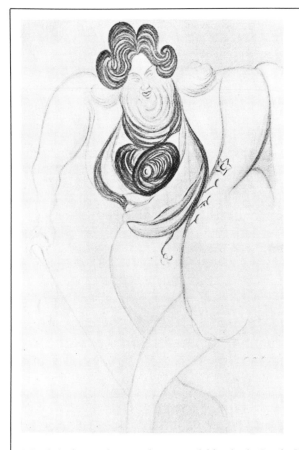
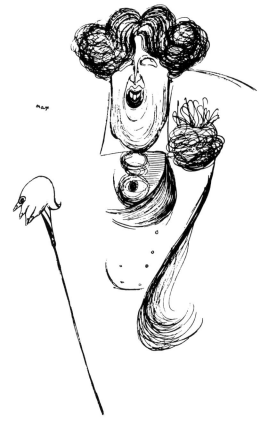

Models from the modern world include Lady Wishfort, the aunts in Saki, Miss Mapp (in the novels of E.F. Benson) and Baroness Ada (Brian Howard's short story).

In a domestic setting, the Phallic Woman may betray her aggression by her clothes. In *My Royal Past: The Memoirs of Baroness von Bülop*, Cecil Beaton describes a triumvirate of Phallic Women:

'My aunt was got up in a malmaison pink *merveilleux* outlined with a chain of coral and jet ladybirds. On her perilously large hat, of harmonising colouring, a diamond sword was thrust through the breast of a flamingo... The Countess Bischoffsheim wore sapphire-blue plush with a short sealskin jacket faced with golden otter... Lady Loins wore fawn and heliotrope shot velvet, the front having stripes of plush, and a lace bonnet trimmed with daffodils and skunk.'

Of the less grotesque Phallic Women, Lady Bracknell is the most celebrated—especially as performed by Dame Edith Evans. Although good at heart, the less grotesque are still overpowering. Even Lady Blanchemain in Henry Harland's wanly camp little novel, *My Friend Prospero*, seems to exude power:

' "It is a good name—there's none better in England," averred the old lady, with a nod of emphasis that set the

George IV and Oscar Wilde by Beerbohm: it seems to be the fate of all who try to imitate Beau Brummell that they end up looking like the Prince Regent.

Opposite page. Top: Diaghilev in the south of France, around 1911. *Bottom:* photographs by Baron von Gloeden of himself and one of his models.

wheatears in her bonnet quivering... And with a great effect of majesty and importance like a conscious thing, her carriage rolled away.'

The Eminence Cerise is a patron of camp culture, an impresario of imposture, a ringmaster of the *recherché*. He organises and pays for camp society, symbolising the camp need for economic support and perhaps at a deeper level the immature failure to break with parental domination. Models include Prinnie, Ludwig II and Diaghilev. These generally rotund figures have something of the monumental about them; they, like the Dandy Wit, are difficult to love. There is also a degree of sexual uncertainty in their cuddly curvaceousness. When a camp person looks at Prinnie, for example, does he not see Mummy peeping out from beneath the wig and peering over the pile of double chins?

Sexual uncertainty plays an important part in the camp preoccupation with youthfulness. 'A thing of beauty,' says Lord Middlebottom in Carl Van Vechten's *The Blind Bow Boy*, 'is a boy forever.' The Beautiful Boy is another camp archetype. By drowning himself in the Nile, the Emperor Hadrian's favourite, Antinous, preserved his youthfulness and made himself an ideal of male beauty. And Dorian Gray's picture was a magic gift that drew all Dorian's ageing into itself, leaving him perpetually youthful. In the

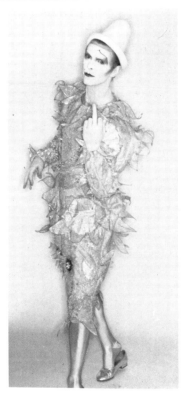

1920s and the 1960s, two decades that saw explosions in camp sensibility, boyishness was adopted as the ideal of female beauty. In the 1920s, women slimmed down, squeezed their breasts and their bottoms flat and cropped their hair; in the 1960s, a decade that produced the foetal beauty of Mia Farrow, the leaders of fashion were a succession of increasingly young-looking girls—Jean Shrimpton, Marianne Faithfull and Twiggy.

Since camp involves a refusal to grow up, it sees ageing as a particularly unattractive process which it is important to carry off with good humour. The actress Mrs Patrick Campbell said of herself that she was 'older than God', and Hermione Gingold, when asked by an immigration officer why she was visiting England, replied: 'To see my two sons both of whom are older than I am.'

The Transvestite represents camp's sexual ambiguity rather than its sexual uncertainty. It has been a constant theme in camp literature from the Abbé de Choisy's story *The Marquise/Marquis de Banneville* and Voiture's poem *Sur sa maîtresse rencontrée en habit de garçon, un soir de carnaval*, through a more extended treatment in Théophile Gautier's *Mademoiselle de Maupin* (a camp *As You Like It*) to the description of Spiridion in Beardsley's *Venus and Tannhäuser*:

'The Virgin was sung by Spiridion, that soft incomparable alto. A miraculous virgin, too, he made of her. To begin with, he dressed the rôle most effectively. His plump legs

Below: the Chevalier d'Eon—as camp as a row of pink tents.

up to the feminine hips of him, were in very white stockings clocked with a false pink. He wore brown kid boots, buttoned to mid-calf and his whorish thighs had thin scarlet garters round them. His jacket was cut like a jockey's, only the sleeves ended in manifold frills, and round the neck, and just upon the shoulders, there was a black cape. His hair was dyed green, was curled into ringlets, such as the smooth Madonnas of Miracles are made lovely with…'

A variation on this archetype, though with music-hall rather than literary origins, is the Burlesque Woman, in whom sexual characteristics are exaggerated to the point of parody. The usual type of the Burlesque Woman is a

man in crude drag, juggling suggestively with balloons, but an interesting variant was provided by Mae West, an American Vaudeville performer, who acted on stage (and later on film) like a female impersonator. She was not an attractive woman—she was heavy-featured and dumpy—but she and everyone else kept up an elaborate pretence that she was irresistible. It is interesting to note that one of her early Broadway stage shows was a celebration of camp homosexuality called *The Drag*. The third and final act of this play had no dialogue, but (*Variety* recorded) there were some thirty young men taking part in the spectacle, 'half tricked-out in women's clothes and half in tuxedos' in an episode that took on 'the character of a chorus girl "pick-out" number in a burlesque show… All hands are rouged, lip-sticked, and liquid-whited to the last degree.' Mae West herself said of homosexuals, 'They're crazy about me 'cause I give 'em a chance to play… It's easy for 'em to imitate me 'cause the gestures are exaggerated, flamboyant, *sexy*, and that's what they wanna look like, feel like, and I've stood up for 'em!' More particularly, Mae West appeals to the sexual timidity in camp, as she divests sex of everything that is dark, dangerous and primeval: under her aegis, it becomes nothing more than a children's romp.

Charles Hawtrey in his underpants as an Indian dancer with Peter Butterworth and Joan Sims in *Carry On…Up the Khyber* (1968).

Opposite: Mae West's burlesque inverts conventional morality: in her world it is not being loved, rather than being loved, that depraves.

A generous amount of contempt is lavished on the archetype of the *Bourgeois Gentilhomme* (and his female equivalent in camp literature. The *Bourgeois Gentilhomme* is at the opposite pole to the Dandy Wit: the butt of camp scorn, a ludicrous figure pretending to wit and style, but totally devoid of them. Models include Vanbrugh's Lady Fanciful and Disraeli's Mrs Million, who remarks that there is nothing like old families, 'with all the awkward feelings of a parvenue'. This archetype features largely in the Bourgeois Macabre genre of camp literature.

Perhaps the earliest example is in Petronius's *The Satyricon*. Written as a parody of *The Odyssey* by Nero's *arbiter elegantiae*, it has titillated camp sensibilities ever since, winning a wider audience when it was first translated into unexpurgated English by Oscar Wilde. If camp writers are naughty boys giggling at the back of the class, *The Satyricon* is the book they have hidden under the desk-lid. The passage that might be labelled Bourgeois Macabre concerns a dinner party given by Trimalchio, a self-important and social-climbing government official. The macabre element is introduced by the food: after the second course a great dish is brought in, supporting an enormous wild boar, with a freedman's cap on its head; from its tusks dangle two baskets woven from palm leaves and filled with

Above: the deliberate courting of neurosis—Audrey Hepburn as Holly Golightly in Blake Edwards's film of Truman Capote's *Breakfast at Tiffany's* (1961). *Left:* Let's do it after the high Roman fashion. *Fellini Satyricon* (1969) points to the similarities between the decadent, disintegrating civilisation of Rome and modern Western Europe.

Cecil Beaton—self portrait.

dates, and positioned all around, as if at its dugs, are little cake piglets. A servant steps forward and plunges a knife into the boar's side, releasing a flock of thrushes. Many of the details of Trimalchio's *Bourgeois Gentilhomme* awfulness are lost on us today but its quality remains familiar through the novels of E.F.Benson and the stage performances of Barry Humphries and Hinge and Brackett.

The Manic Poseur or Poseuse (examples: Anthony Blanche in *Brideshead Revisited*, Holly Golightly in *Breakfast at Tiffany's*, Sally Bowles in *Goodbye to Berlin/Cabaret*) represents the attempt to glamorise neurosis. Expression, it is well-known, gives temporary relief to neurosis, but persistent expression does more than relieve:

The young Rex Whistler photographed by Cecil Beaton.

The Marchesa Casati arrived at Man
Ray's studio one day, and demanded
to be photographed. 1930s.

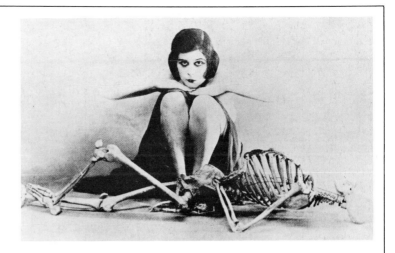

'Such great jambons of knees!' (Firbank). A publicity still of Theda Bara for *A Fool There Was* (1914).

neurosis undergoes a tacky sort of transfiguration. According to Lionel Trilling in *Sincerity and Authenticity*, Denis Diderot's dialogue, *Rameau's Nephew*, was the first detailed account of a person totally immersed in inauthenticity. The interlocutor does not know what to make of the outrageous behaviour, the alternately true and false notions, and the total perversion of feeling expressed with uncommon candour; the Nephew is a knot of contradictions. 'Nothing,' says Diderot, 'is more unlike him than himself'. The contradictory nature of the Manic Poseur's personality is the determining principle of his or her self-presentation.

If you had been taking a midnight stroll in the 1890s along one of the damp narrow passages that lead off St Mark's Square in Venice, you might suddenly have found yourself face to face with a tall, thin woman with wild, black hair, snow-white skin, heavily made-up eyes and cheek-bones like knives; she might have been walking a black panther on a leash. If you had escorted her home, you would have arrived at a half-built palace overlooking a canal, half-lit by braziers refuelled by naked slaves and decorated with portraits of the hostess by fashionable artists of the day, such as Alastair and Boldini. Guests at the palazzo might have included René Lalique and Paul Poiret, both of whom designed their most inspired creations for this most scandalous and notorious of women.

She was the Marchesa Casati, who perfected the archetype of the Vamp. Other models include Cleopatra (especially as portrayed by Ida Rubenstein), Swinburne's Dolores and Aldous Huxley's heroine Myra Viveash, who 'speaks in a faint and husky voice as if each breath were her last.' Theda Bara, who played the Vamp in such masterpieces as *The Tiger Woman* and *When Men Desire*, was liable to pose for publicity stills gloating over the skeletons of her victims; in *A Fool There Was*, she plays a heartless hussy who reduces a top diplomat to a drivelling wreck, whom she bestrides, triumphantly sneering 'Kiss me, fool!'—she was a particular fad of Ronald Firbank's.

The Vamp does not have the welcoming, malleable properties of a sex object. She is rather, a sex subject, sharp, angular and predatory. In the sex war, she carries the fighting to the men. Though they may toy with the idea, there are few things that men find more unpleasant or more uncomfortable than the sensation of being desired. Few men have the assurance for self-surrender. It is this possibility, part-thrilling and part-horrifying, that the Vamp represents. The stare of the Vamp turns men not to stone but to meat.

Brighton Pavilion. Brigid Brophy has pointed out the evident influence that the curves and flourishes of Brighton's architecture had on the linear style of the young Aubrey Beardsley, who lived there.

Since the overwhelming interest of camp literature is in human relations, in admiration and envy, and in reputations won and lost, landscape plays little part in it. Where it does feature, it is in the form of a highly fanciful version of the picturesque. Here it sets off nicely Disraeli's fictional alter ego:

'It was an autumnal night, the wind was capricious and changeable as a petted beauty, or an Italian greyhound, or a shot silk. Now the breeze blew so fresh that the white clouds dashed along the sky as if they bore a band of witches too late for their Sabbath meeting. Vivian Grey was leaning against an old beech tree in the most secluded part of the park, and was gazing at the moon.'

Saki can only bear to contemplate landscape if it is turned into an extension of the drawing room:

'There were lots of other delightful things in the park. There were ponds with gold and blue and green fish in them, and trees with beautiful parrots that said clever things at a moment's notice, and humming birds that hummed all the popular tunes of the day.' (*The Story Teller*.)

Even when it ventures outdoors, camp is less concerned with the joys of nature than with the allure of style. Since

The Pagoda in the Royal Gardens at Kew, designed by Sir William Chambers, who did much to popularise oriental styles in the eighteenth century. In *The Art of Laying Out Gardens Among the Chinese*, he described Chinese buildings as 'toys in architecture...acceptable because of their oddity.' 'Novelty' he decided 'sometimes takes the place of beauty.'

they shy away from the established social order, it is natural that the camp should spurn established styles. Marginal styles that especially recommend themselves as camp fads do not have any strong ideological impact or social relevance to the imposition of camp meanings; they are styles that invite a degree of condescension.

Distance in space, time or class enables the camp to see a style as marginal, irrelevant or quaint, adjectives applicable respectively to the camp fads for exoticism, revivalism and *nostalgie de la boue*.

'Irony,' said Marcel Duchamp, 'is a playful way of accepting something.' Camp accepts alien styles in a playful way, so that they express a gleeful sense of alienation from the establishment. The Orient interpreted as a place of reckless splendour, of effeminate luxury and strange sexual indulgences, has been a major subject for camp exploitation, its exotic styles seeming to offer a delightful alternative to the stodgy life-style of the bourgeoisie.

The most famous cod-Oriental building in England is the Brighton Pavilion. Camp's approach to styles characteristically shows little regard for their real ideological origins. We should not inquire too deeply into the various styles on show in the Pavilion (a mishmash of Turkish, Tartar, Hindu and Chinese), because its designers didn't. In it, Prinnie held lavish entertainments. In his imposing Field Marshal's uniform, he channelled his tactical talents into organising the footmen who were serving iced champagne punch, Sauternes and soda water, and sherbert. A worthy member of Parliament complained in the House that the Pavilion showed 'more of the pomp and magnificence of a Persian satrap in all the splendour of Oriental state than the sober dignity of a British prince,' which is presumably pretty much what it was intended to show.

Disraeli also enjoyed the Oriental. Travelling *comme d'habitude* in fancy dress—a blood-red shirt with silver studs, a scarf for a girdle, and red slippers—he visited the Turkish Grand Vizier and wrote back to England describing archly 'the delight of being made much of by a man who was daily decapitating half the province.'

Ludwig II dabbled in the Oriental among many other styles. Perhaps his major contribution to camp exoticism was his Moorish kiosk at the Lunderhof castle, which was erected in 1877 and furnished with a dazzling peacock throne, made for him in Paris by Le Blanc-Granger.

In the twentieth century, the man most involved in spreading the camp taste for the exotic was Diaghilev. His powerfully exotic productions—*Scheherazade*, *Cleopatra* (starring Ida Rubenstein) and *Le Spectre de la Rose*—and especially their designs by Alexandre Benois and Léon Bakst, influenced many branches of the decorative arts. Martin Battersby has traced Diaghilev's influence in the fashion designs of Poiret, Cartier brooches, the pungent

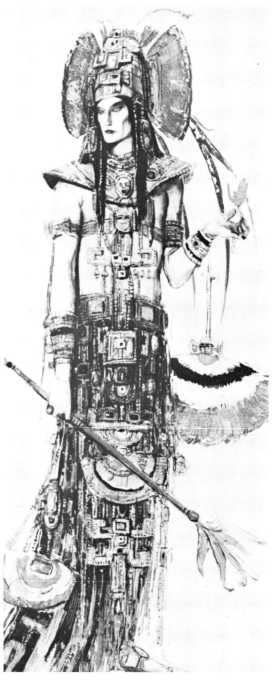

perfumes of the time, and in the richer and more sultry colours that began to seep into European drawing rooms; he even identified it in things as far removed as the Ziegfeld Follies and the films of Busby Berkeley.

At the first night performance of *Scheherazade* in Paris, one scene in particular provoked a happy response from an audience that included, among other celebrities, Robert de Montesquiou and Jean Cocteau. In it, the ladies of the harem, while their husband is away, throw themselves on a group of muscular negroes.

Left: A deliciously decadent costume design by Léon Bakst for Ethel Levey, a vaudeville actress who performed in *Hello Tango* at the London Hippodrome in 1913. *Right:* costume design by Charles Ricketts for *Montezuma*, c1925.

Later, with the popularisation of some of the more accessible parts of jazz and the craze for dances such as the Black Bottom, the camp vogue for the primitive centred in Paris on the dancer, Josephine Baker ('La Bakaire'), a self-parodying black sex-symbol, one of whose costumes was made entirely out of bananas. In London, the American show troupe, The Blackbirds, were fêted by Brian Howard and the Bright Young Things. In literature, the half-fascinated, half-fearful reaction of camp people to negroes found expression in Ronald Firbank's *Valmouth*:

'By the little garden pergola open to the winds some fluttered peacocks were blotted nervelessly amid the dripping trees, their heads sunk back beneath their wings: while in the pergola itself, like a fallen storm cloud, lolled a negress, her levelled, polecat eyes semi-veiled by the nebulous alchemy of the rainbow.

"What are you doing fiddle-faddling over there, Elizabeth?" Mrs Hurstpierpoint asked.

"Look, Eulalia," Mrs Thoroughfare said, catching her breath; "someone with a kite is on our lawn!"
Mrs Hurstpierpoint was impelled to smile.

"In the old days," she murmured, brushing a few crumbs from her gown, "sailing a kite heavenward was my utmost felicity. No ball of string, I remember, was ever long enough!"

"This is no Christian and her kite, Eulalia, or I'm much mistaken..."

"No Christian, Elizabeth?"

"It's a savage."
Mrs Hurstpierpoint sank humbly to her knees.
"Gloria in Excelsis tibi Deo!" she solemnly exclaimed.'

One of the ways in which mankind progresses is by idealising the past and then attempting to recreate it. Camp employs a perversion of this process in which idealised versions of the past are recreated with the intention of

Above: Josephine Baker, whose performances showed a camp fusion of the comic and the erotic. *Right:* The Stray Cats—'fifties revivalism in the 1980s.

Whimsically anachronistic, singer Mari Wilson recycles the fashions of the 1960s.

being retrograde rather than progressive. Camp takes styles from the past and uses them to sidestep the onward march of history. The historical is reduced to the ephemeral.

An early example of camp revivalism was Horace Walpole's Gothic Revival in the eighteenth century. Here he writes a letter about his plans for his Gothic castle at Strawberry Hill:

'Twickenham June 8 1747
You perceive by my date that I am got into a new camp, and have left my tub at Windsor. It is a little plaything-house that I got out of Mrs Chenevin's shop, and is the prettiest bauble you ever saw. It is set in enamelled meadows, with filigree hedges... Two delightful roads, that you would call dusty, supply me continually with coaches and chaises... Dowagers as plenty as flounders inhabit all around, and Pope's ghost is just now skimming under my window by a most poetical moonlight.'

All the decorative little battlements and turrets impart an air of dinkiness to Strawberry Hill. The darkness and power of Gothic has been extracted so that what is left is an elaborate camp joke—Gothick. Where Gothic symbolised spirituality, Gothick negated it.

We have already noted other examples of camp revivalism in Monsieur's adopting the style of Henri III and Oscar Wilde's neo-Regency. Since the 1960s, with pop culture

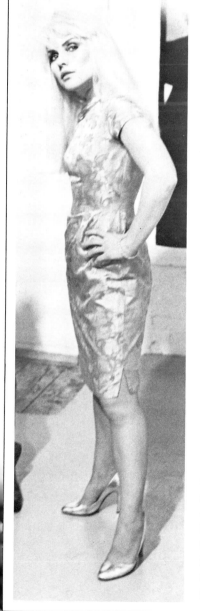

Right: Edith Sitwell posing in imitation of a Zoffany conversation piece at Renishaw Hall in 1927. *Below:* Debbie Harry, who was a waitress at Max's, Kansas City while it was Andy Warhol's headquarters. Blondie, her mock bubble-gum pop group, presents itself with a sense of irony that is still recognisably Warholesque.

espousing Victoriana, revivalism has dominated popular fashion. We have had revivals of 'twenties, 'thirties, 'forties, 'fifties and now even 'sixties styles. Again, the revivals are indifferent to the ideological meanings of the styles, which are prized rather for their marginality and thus their novelty.

A feature of this permutation of camp, as Michael Wood explained in 'An Anatomy of Rubbish' in *New Society*, is that the things chosen for fads must have become *démodé*, or at least have ceased to be in the vanguard of culture, but they must not yet be old enough to be of interest to antiquarians or social historians. Writing in 1969, Wood gave the examples of co-respondent shoes and the double-breasted suits of the 1930s, which were just passing out of camp fashion, and the WRAC overcoats of the 1940s, which were just coming in.

Camp thrives where High Life meets Low Life: in the New York discos, for example, where socialites and media celebrities mix with Andy Warhol's transvestite superstars. Some of Robert de Montesquiou's favourite stories concerned a duchess who was 'so devoted to the ideal of beauty that she looked for it in her footman, and found it there.' 'If Madame would be so good as to move a little further over to the left thigh, then I would have the honour of giving Her Grace the more enjoyment' the footman is supposed to have remarked.

In the camp persona, *nostalgie de la boue* expresses itself in the mixture of elegance and crudity. It is the raucous element in camp that keeps it from fading away altogether, as it is constantly threatening to in its more courtly and cerebral forms. We find elegance plus crudity in, for instance, Beardsley's drawings and in Beckford's *Vathek*:

'The city re-echoed with shouts of joy and flourishing of trumpets. Nothing was visible but plumes nodding on pavilions, and aigrets shining in the mild lustre of the moon. The spacious square resembled an immense parterre variegated with the most stately tulips of the East.
'Arrayed in the robes which were only worn at the most distinguished ceremonials, and supported by his vizier and Bababalouk, the caliph descended the great staircase of the tower in the sight of all his people. For some time a general stillness prevailed, which nothing happened to disturb but the shrill screams of some eunuchs in the rear. These vigilant guards, having remarked certain cages of the ladies swagging somewhat awry, and discovered that a few adventurous gallants had contrived to get in, soon dislodged the enraptured culprits, and consigned them, with good commendations, to the surgeons of the serail.'

Raquel Welch (Andy Warhol's favourite film star) in *One Million Years BC*.

The American wrestler Gorgeous George used to refuse to wrestle on canvas that had not been sprayed with Chanel perfume. He entered the ring to the sound of a Pomp and Circumstance march. Then his valet would remove his gold hair net to let down his long blond hair. When the referee tried to run his hands down each wrestler's body, checking for illegal use of grease, the Human Orchid refused to let himself be touched. The crowd would roar. 'I don't think I'm gorgeous,' said George, 'but what's my opinion against millions of others?'

Other artistic manifestations of *nostalgie de la boue* are to be found in the fads of the Good/Bad and the So-Bad-It's-Good, and in the Trash aesthetic. It is by no means a new idea, e.g.:

'Well, for my part,' said Mr Berners, 'I do not like your suburban dinners. You always get something you can't eat, and cursed bad wine.'
'I rather like bad wine,' said Mr Mountchesney; 'one gets so bored with good wine.' (Disraeli, *Sybil*, 1845)

'The man of intelligence, who will never agree with anyone, should cultivate a pleasure in the conversation of imbeciles and the study of worthless books. From these he will derive a sardonic amusement which will largely repay him for his pains.' (Baudelaire, *Journals*, 1860).

George Orwell gave voice to the fad for the Good/Bad in an essay of 1945, in which he put the case for books without literary pretensions that nevertheless were more readable than more ambitious productions. 'Not inhibited by good

Zsa Zsa Gabor in the title rôle of
Queen of Outer Space (1958).

taste' books such as the Raffles and Sherlock Holmes
stories, *King Solomon's Mines* and *Dracula*, showed pure
skill and 'native grace' in their writing. *Uncle Tom's Cabin*
was in Orwell's eyes the supreme example of an unintentionally ludicrous book, which 'one's intellect simply re-
fuses to take seriously' but which still excites and even
moves.

By arguing in the same essay that some music hall songs
made better poems than most of the seriously intended
poems in the published anthologies, Orwell widened the
horizons of the Good/Bad faddists. The fad spread to the
stylised unreality of comics and cartoons, to various mass-
produced artefacts such as comic seaside postcards and
cigarette cards, and to what has been perhaps the richest
source of the Good/Bad in the cinema. Good/Bad films
with great camp appeal have included *Casablanca*, *The
Devil Is a Woman* and *King Kong*.

Closely related to Good/Bad films, but distinguishable
from them are So-Bad-That-They're-Good films. Truly
awful films such as *Godzilla Meets The Thing*, *One Million
Years BC* or *Butterfield 8* raise howls of *ersatz* delight from
a camp audience.

As an audience became recognisable, purposefully
Good/Bad, i.e. camp, films began to be produced. American underground films in particular have made great play
with camp themes—exhibitionism, transvestism, deliberate over-acting and something that Parker Tyler called

Kenneth Anger's film *The Inauguration of the Pleasure Dome* (1954).

conscious condescension towards the vulgar as a source of value.' Kenneth Anger's *The Inauguration of the Pleasure Dome* (three versions: 1954, 1958, 1966) portrays a party hosted by a figure of changeable sexuality, who varies clothes and personality to greet each new guest—a Marilyn blonde, an African goddess and Cesare (the somnambulist from *The Cabinet of Dr Caligari*). Anger's film *Scorpio Rising* (1963) celebrates macho camp: in one scene, a bikeboy dresses himself in studded leather and chains while Bobby Vinton sings 'She wore blue velvet'—a quintessentially camp juxtaposition. Another Anger film, *Kustom Kar Kommandoes* (1965), includes a blond Californian boy dusting his hot-rod with a powder-puff. Jack Smith's *Flaming Creatures* (1963) is a film of a transvestite orgy, set in a Tangiers drag club.

Some underground fims, such as *The Queen of Sheba Meets the Atom Man* and *Sins of the Fleshapoids*, parodied the science fiction comic-strips of the 'thirties and 'forties that had been Good/Bad camp fads. Another prominent

Below and left: Jack Smith's film *Flaming Creatures* (1963).

Mike Kuchar's film *Sins of the Fleshapoids* (1965).

feature of these underground films has been their parody of old Hollywood stereotypes: Warhol's *Mario Banana* (1964) has Mario Montez parodying a marginal Hollywood star, and *Lonesome Cowboys* (1968) burlesques the homosexuality that is seen to be latent in the traditional gun fights and tussles of the Western; *Heat* (1972) contains a parody of the murder scene in *Sunset Boulevard*.

Through the 'sixties and into the 'seventies, the elements of camp nostalgia and parody were also to be found in commercial cinema and television, e.g. *Whatever Happened to Baby Jane? Modesty Blaise, Barbarella, Batman, The Avengers, The Man From U.N.C.L.E., Adam Adamant* and *Jason King*.

Below: John Phillip Law as the Angel in Roger Vadim's *Barbarella* (1968). *Right:* Batman and Robin in the original movie serial. After its camp following had been recognised, the television version was made deliberately camp.

Parallel to the camp fads for the Good/Bad and the So-Bad-It's-Good in literature and films, the Trash Aesthetic developed in sculpture and in painting.

The dandified Marcel Duchamp was the first artist to recognise camp possibilities in the aesthetic exploitation of the mass-produced artefacts of the consumer society with his infamous ready-mades; when asked on an American chat show what he liked about America, he said that he liked the plumbing. Duchamp's campness extended into cross-sexual posturing. He adopted the pseudonym Rrose Selavy and included a Man Ray photograph of himself in drag on a perfume bottle label titled *Belle Haleine, Eau de Voillette* (1921).

In 1965, Thomas B. Hess wrote of Duchamp:

'He has that interior-decorator's eye which spots beautiful items in the dingiest flea-market. When Duchamp sent a commonplace or despicable object to an art exhibition (the hat-rack or the urinal, i.e. the 'ready-mades'), it was an anti-art gesture at modern sculpture, but the additional twist for his fan-club was that the object really *is* beautiful in itself... In this sly way, Camp Art was born... Camp Art

Belle Haleine. This joint work by Marcel Duchamp and Man Ray features Duchamp in drag photographed by Ray. The wording on the label is teasingly ambiguous.

is perfect expression of the artist as man of the world. It is trivial because of its reliance on a built-in audience; it exists in the smirk of the beholder.'

He describes Duchamp as having a 'sort of dainty talent' and says of his use of colour that it is 'superficially garish'—though one might wonder how anything could be deeply garish.

Duchamp's great importance in the history of the development of camp was that he isolated and used in the most uncompromising and unadulterated way camp's ironic reflection both on the marginal (in this case the trashy) and on the person who is committed to the marginal (either the artist himself or anyone who applied himself to appreciating Duchamp's sculptures as art).

It was a development which was to be popularised some forty years later by Pop Artists, such as Duchamp's friend and disciple, Richard Hamilton, and, of course, by Andy Warhol.

In the meantime, the mainstream of art was moving in a different directon. Surrealism, various forms of primitivism and later American Abstract Expressionism became the orthodoxy. What all elements in this orthodoxy shared was a belief in one form or other in the surrealist doctrine of the 'omnipotence of the dream', the idea that if you reached far enough down into the subconscious, you would find images that, being archetypal and therefore present in everyone's subconscious, would strike some sort of chord. Camp art arose at a time when it was becoming apparent that an entirely subjective and spontaneous mode of painting couldn't be sustained without loss of vigour and incisiveness; art that did not feed on the diversity of the material world ended by feeding on itself. The original surrealists had invited artists to explore the subconscious, which they presented as one big playground of infinite variety and strangeness, but once the invitation had been accepted, it all disintegrated in a farrago of depressingly familiar clichés and stereotypes—the ruin, the monster, the monolith, the hybrid and all the other stalwarts of 'imaginative' art and literature.

This process of disillusionment was heightened by the fashion for hallucinogenic drugs, which had been favoured by surrealists as a passport to wonderland. Drug takers had been led to expect that they would be confronted by mythical creatures from the depths of the subconscious. In fact, when the doors of perception swung open, they found themselves faced with the mental driftwood that floats on the top of the mind. At the same time, psychologists were becoming increasingly suspicious of the idea that, deep down in the subconscious, there was some sort of common ground, some sort of collective unconscious; without this, there was no reason to think that these highly subjective paintings could convey meaning to anyone other than the artist who had painted them. In a famous interview in 1947, Jackson Pollock said that when he was 'in his painting' he was not aware of what he was doing, and by 1957 more and more people had come to agree with him.

Disenchantment with the self-indulgent soul-searching of the artists' current orthodoxy was accompanied by a disdain for the personal style—their beards, their sandals and all the other outward expressons of crushing sincerity. An important factor in this new mood, and one which was to play a big part in the new camp movement in art, was the growing popularity of jazz among white people, and their subsequent appropriation of the black concept of cool, already reflected and even to an extent anticipated by such cool-but-white stars as Humphrey Bogart and Veronica Lake. Cool was affectlessness made chic: it made a virtue out of being blank. Like a very vulgarised version of the Englishman's stiff upper lip (and speaking in similarly truncated sentences), cool characterised emotion as an embarrassment. Cool gave nothing away by word or action, never left itself vulnerable. The quintessentially cool person cruised into town wearing sunglasses, usually the kind that merely mirrored an inquiring glance.

Andy Warhol was the leading figure in the movement that reacted against the mainstream art of the time. Where his predecessors had been introspective, he was impersonal; where they had been imaginative, he was a realist; where they had been earnest, he was flip; where they had been emotive, he was cool. He fused these elements together to create the first strongly American version of camp.

Standing in front of a Warhol painting is in many ways like meeting a camp person: the painting is so outrageous as immediately to command our attention; its colours are brash and discordant, its subject matter trivial and trashy. We try to apply received notions of art appreciation and none of them seems quite to fit. We are uncomfortably aware all the time that the artist may be laughing at us for even beginning to take him so seriously. The painting doesn't allow the mind to settle, but sets it off on a series of questions, a complex interchange of implication and denial that operates on several levels:

How can a soup tin be the subject matter for a work of art?
If a soup tin can be the subject matter for a work of art, is a soup tin more beautiful than I have noticed?
If a soup tin can be said to be beautiful, should I reconsider my notion of beauty?
Does this soup tin have any meaning?
If a soup tin in an art gallery can be said to have meaning, is the same true of a soup tin in a supermarket?
If this soup tin is supposed to be ugly, is the artist trying to make me more aware of the ugliness that surrounds me in the supermarket?

Soup Can by Andy Warhol.

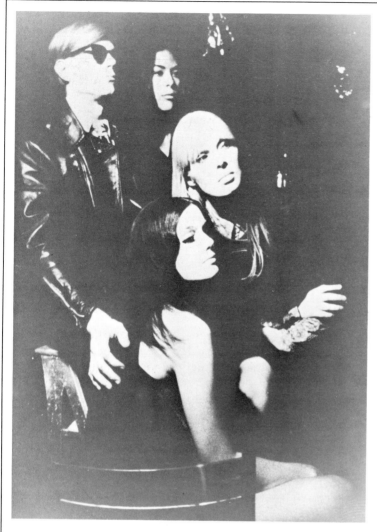

Andy Warhol with Nico when he was directing *Chelsea Girls* (1966). In *A to B and Back Again, the Philosophy of Andy Warhol*, he mischievously wonders why he was never an abstract expressionist; with his unsteady hands, he muses, he would have been a natural.

Is the artist denigrating art or the state of art today?
Am I supposed to invest this painting with my own meaning?
If I am, it seems to me that I am doing all the work; in that case, what am I doing here?
If I am doing all the work, have I the wherewithal to be an artist?

In this way, Warhol made use of the many layers of irony that camp had built up over the centuries to refine sensory perception to a state of maximum self-awareness. Camp is raised here to the level of the highest artistic and intellectual seriousness. As in Duchamp's work, the unresolved ambiguities and the reverberating ironies that had formerly been only incidental features of camp art now became its rationale.

A star of chat shows and gossip columns, Warhol was also an extremely popular artist, perhaps the most celebrated in the world. His version of camp took as its subject matter mass production and media heroes— people's work

Camp comics now regularly appear on television and in films. American comedienne and singer Bette Midler has achieved international success ith a camp mixture of sexual burlesque, kitsch exploitation and the reviving of period songs.

Sultry Elvis Presley and well-scrubbed Dolores Hart in *Loving You* (1957).

and leisure. Unlike Duchamp's, it owed little to the genteel traditions of the art world. It managed to be anti-establishment and at the same time unaligned with the elitist anti-establishment tradition of which the Abstract Expressionists were the latest representatives. Warhol aligned himself rather with the lower strata of society. He was, then, the perfect person to carry the gift of camp from the small, over-educated cliques to the people, and, unlikely Prometheus though he might seem, that is what he did.

The medium of this popularisation was not to be painting or even films (unsuitable because of their high-brow connotations) but pop music. Pop music has always contained an element of camp. We need only think of three of the most influential figures in pop, Elvis Presley in the 'fifties, Mick Jagger in the 'sixties and David Bowie in the 'seventies, to see how this camp element has increased.

The gloriously stupid Elvis Presley had a Jean Cocteau profile, gold lamé suits, mascara and a moody black quiff. Singing 'You can do anything, but don't step on my blue suede shoes', he introduced to pop a camp concern with the minutiae of personal appearance. He would swivel his hips like Rita Hayworth, and his voice was as suggestive as Mae West's. In an Anglo Saxon world, where only women flaunted their sexuality, effeminacy was the best course open to a male sex symbol—even the frumpish Bill Haley sported a kiss curl. By 1959, pop had passed into its high school or soda pop phase, with Fabian, Frankie Avalon, Connie Francis and Lesley Gore, when record producers of Machiavellian ambitions set about marketing music for teenagers filled with teen traumas at beach parties and drive-in movies. Some of the more talented producers who were aware of the absurd side of pop, such as Phil Spector,

The Shangri Las translated stories from cartoons for pubescent girls into records. The mock naivety of these teen operas has always endeared them to camp.

couldn't help camping things up. The Shangri-las' *Past, Present and Future*, produced by Shadow Morton, was a camp classic. The lyric is breathily intoned over a Mantovani-style arrangement of the 'Moonlight' sonata:

'The Past. The past, well now, let me tell you about the past. The Past is filled with silent joys and broken toys, laughing girls and teasing boys. Was I ever in love? I called it love. I mean it felt like love. There were moments when...well, there were moments when...

'The Present. Go out with you? Why not. Do I like to dance? Of course. Take a walk along the beach tonight? I'd love to, but don't try to touch me, don't try to touch me, 'cos that will never happen again. Shall we dance? [At this point the music changes and swirls off into a waltz.]

'The Future. Tomorrow. Well, tomorrow is a long way off. Maybe someday I'll hold somebody's hand, maybe somewhere someone will understand. You know, I used to sing "A tisket, a tasket, a green and yellow basket. I'm all packed up and I'm on my way, and gonna fall in love." But at the moment it doesn't look good. At the moment it'll never happen again. I don't think it will ever happen again'

P.J. Proby minced onstage in a Little Boy Blue velveteen suit, a ribbon in his hair and a hand on his hip. He'd sing soulful ballads with a rasping satirical voice, and imitate

P.J. Proby's vanity was such that he had to be the centre of attention or nowhere at all. His self-destructive exhibitionism led eventually to his being barred from most theatres and from the BBC and consequently to bankruptcy.

the ecstatic facial expressions of his fans. 'What kind of fool am I,' he lisped, 'What kind of lips are these that lied with every kiss, that whispered wempty words of love and left me alone like this?' Nik Cohn's novel *I am still the greatest says Johnny Angelo*, gives a highly colourful fictionalised account not only of Proby's stage act, but also of his mythomaniac fantasies.

In the years following 1963, England retaliated. The Beatles and other groups were ex-art-school boys who knew what an effective weapon camp could be. They had studied Richard Hamilton and the other English pop artists. Wearing old military uniforms, Granny spectacles and Victorian nightdresses, the English groups and their girlfriends conquered the world in a camp re-run of England's earlier imperialist expansion. Drake's drum was heard again, but this time laying down the beat in a rock 'n'

Just What Is It That Makes Today's Homes So Different So Appealing? by Richard Hamilton, disciple of Marcel Duchamp and teacher of Bryan Ferry. His work embodies the close relationship between camp art and camp pop.

Mick Jagger, Brian Jones,
Charlie Watts and Bill Wyman of The
Rolling Stones arriving in Italy at the
start of a concert tour, 1967.

Opposite: Mick Jagger's stage
performance squeezes from camp
every last possible drop of lubricity.

roll band. Mick Jagger wriggled and pouted, not so much
playing the game as on the game. James Bond, by far the
most popular screen hero of the decade, was a direct de-
scendant of Alan Quartermain, Richard Hannay and all
the other heroes of Empire, except that he liked sex and
stuff like that—the mores of a new empire whose empress
was not the Queen but Princess Margaret. Twiggy and
Dave Clark replaced Jayne Mansfield and John Wayne as
the ideal bodies. The vogue word of the time was kinky,
with its camp overtones of fetishism. A camp group called
The Kinks, who appeared on the scene in red hunting coats
and sang in mock upper-class accents, recorded the song
that perhaps best captured the spirit of Swinging London:

> They seek him here
> They seek him there.
> His clothes are loud
> But never square.
> It will make or break him
> So he stops to buy the best,
> Because he's a dedicated follower of fashion.

> And when he does his little rounds
> Round the boutiques of London Town

Ray Davies of The Kinks. 'Boys will be girls and girls will be boys.'

Eagerly pursuing all the latest fads and trends
Because he's a dedicated follower of fashion.

He thinks he is a flower to be looked at
And when he pulls his frilly nylon panties
Right up tight,
He feels a dedicated follower of fashion.

There's one thing that he loves
And that is flattery.
One week he's in polka dots,
The next week he's in stripes,
'Cos he's a dedicated follower of fashion.

They seek him here
They seek him there
In Regent's Street
And Leicester Square
Everywhere the Carnabetian army marches on
Each one a dedicated follower of fashion...

Not only could the least affluent person in England now afford to be a fop and dandy, but he also had the inclination. As George Melly (himself a camp performer of some panache) points out in his book, *Revolt Into Style*, camp

Duggie Fields with one of his paintings, which juxtapose glamorous accessories with crude 'pop' colours and stock images from art history.

divested itself of the narrowly homosexual connotations that it had acquired in the early part of the century. The spirited, colourful pageant of English pop culture (the Union Jacks, World Cup Willie, the Lord Kitchener posters) was the attempt of a generation to find its identity, to come to terms with its heritage, an enterprise involving that mixture of cynicism and sentimentality, mockery and nostalgia which is characteristically camp.

In the late 'sixties, the movement lost the irreverence and the playfulness that are among camp's better qualities. One reason was the growing isolation of the established pop stars from their audiences, but another lay in the particular brand of camp they had been exposed to at art school. English Pop Art had a gentility, a whimsicality and a tendency to understatement that suits Englishmen but not Pop Art. The American paintings had an appropriately cinematic scale and an all-important crudity which the English could never bring themselves to copy. In the camp mixture of cynicism and sentimentality, the English exhibited an imbalance in favour of sentimentality that seriously weakened their potency. English pop stars also began to look outside pop for their philosophy: in a search for something misleadingly called credibility, they placed themselves at the end of a tradition of protest in highbrow art and literature. Seen from an ideological rather than a sociological viewpoint, pop (or rock, as it was now called) was not merely the exploitation of the unprecedented amount of money that had fallen into the hands of teen-agers since the 1950s, but a serious artistic to come to terms with life lived under the threat of the Bomb. Understandably, rock music produced within this frame of reference was unbearably pompous.

The English groups (now bands) grew paunches, which they wore like Victorian patriarchs as symbols of their self-satisfaction. They and their American imitators lost the art of writing the short, snappy singles that had made them famous. Most of them indulged in a sort of insipid pseudo-orientalism that had all the kitsch of *The Mikado* and none of its humour. During one of Led Zeppelin's interminable drum solos, a whole new generation of teen-agers grew up. They remembered neither of the great pop revolutions of 1956 and 1963. Watching *Rock Around The Clock* on the television in the spring of 1970, it was difficult to believe that it had ever inspired kids to rip up cinema seats out of anything other than sheer listlessness, and if, as elder brothers claimed, Mungo Jerry were commercial rubbish, what was so different about 'She loves you, yeah, yeah, yeah'?

It was in response to the atmosphere of torpor and self-indulgence that Andy Warhol effected his second camp coup—a distant and down-market echo of his origin-al revolt against the Abstract Expressionists in 1961. Rock had grown too subjective to have mass appeal; nirvana had been promised to drug-takers by new demagogues (most notably Timothy Leary), and a new generation had duly been disappointed; rock had lost its cool by becoming earnest.

When Glam Rock arrived in 1970, it had none of the quaint, home-made charm of the camp that had been fil-tered through English Pop Art. It was brash, swishy and obvious. The first Glam Rock performer to break through was the ex-Underground star Marc Bolan. He flounced onstage with glitter on his face and hair, and pranced and posed like P.J. Proby's younger sister. In his make-up, he was truly pretty. It was even rumoured that he was to undergo a sex-change operation. People died in accidents at his concerts, the taxmen cornered him, and all the other trappings of superstardom accrued to him. He sold more records in English rock than anyone since the Beatles. Balding old hippies emerged from behind their pints of real ale to see that their toddlers had abandoned the push-chair, and were now clambering on ten inch platform boots after the pert, satin-clad buttocks of their arch-betrayer. It was the time of the first generation gap in rock. Svelte David Bowie, self-styled Leper Messiah, took his lead from Bolan and made much play of his bisexuality in the

Opposite: David Bowie has experimented with many different brands of camp from the brassy outrage of his Ziggy Stardust days to something much more dandified. Chicago, 1975.

Left: Marc Bolan, self-styled dandy in the underworld. *Below:* Blind Jack, a member of Lindsay Kemp & Company, in a performance at the Bush Theatre, Shepherd's Bush, London, in 1975. Mime artist Lindsay Kemp is perhaps best known for his influence on David Bowie, but his own work, including versions of Oscar Wilde's *Salomé* and Jean Genet's *Notre Dame des Fleurs*, features astonishing stage images, far outside the range of rock concerts.

press. 'Everyone is bisexual' became the cliché of the day, and homosexuality, far from not daring to speak its name, was absolutely *de rigueur*. 'The music should be tarted up', said Bowie, 'made into a parody of itself. It should be the clown, the Pierrot medium.' Paul Raven, ageing rock and roll star, sank a coffin full of his old, unsuccessful records in the Thames, and began a new career as Gary Glitter: 'Do you wanna touch me?'
'Where?'
'There!'
'Oh yeah!' sang the fans.
Suzi Quatro, the Modesty Blaise of rock, squeezed into black leather and appeared on television with a cosmetic bruise on her face. Perhaps the best song of the movement was *In Every Dreamhome a Heartache* by Bryan Ferry of Roxy Music. A man in love with an inflatable doll was a witty variant on the camp theme of commitment to the unworthy. The subject matter illustrates how camp in

Opposite page. Left: Rock star Gary Glitter carries it off. *Right:* Suzi Quatro. In their invitations to sado-masochism, her leather costumes were reminiscent of the camp kinkiness of the 1960s as embodied, for example, in *Modesty Blaise*, and by Emma Peel in *The Avengers*.

the 'seventies became less a way of coming to terms with the past and more a way of coming to terms with the trash culture of the moment. For European rock, this meant considering the problem of being fake-Americans—ironic in view of the fact that pop art, as originated in America, was an attempt by artists there to stop being what F. Scott Fitzgerald had termed 'fake-Europeans'.

In every dreamhome a heartache,
And every step I take
Takes me further from heaven.
Is there a heaven?
I'd like to think so.

Standards of living,
They're rising daily,
But 'Home, oh sweet home'
It's only a saying.
From bell-push to faucet
In smart town apartment,
The cottage is pretty,
The main house a palace,
Penthouse perfection
But what goes on?
What to do there?
Better pray there.

Open-plan living
Bungalow ranch style
All of its comforts
Seem so essential
I bought you mail order,
My plain wrapper baby,
Your skin is like vinyl,
The perfect companion
You float in my new pool,
De-luxe and delightful.
Inflatable doll,
My role is to serve you.
Disposable darling,
Can't throw you away now.
Immortal and life-size,
My breath is inside you.
I'll dress you up daily
And keep you till death sighs.
Inflatable doll,
Lover ungrateful,
I blew up your body
But you blew my mind!

Other stars of Glam Rock were Elton John (a sort of Rockin' Hockney), Alvin Stardust, Alice Cooper, Mott the Hoople, The New York Dolls, Mud, The Sweet, Cockney Rebel and Queen. Some wore the gear better than others; The Sweet, who were big lads with lumpy faces, looked like apprentice pantomime dames.

The acknowledged prime mover of Glam Rock was Lou Reed, the Warhol superstar who became a real superstar, a pop music projection of Warhol himself. The story of his arrival as a young boy at Warhol's sleazy HQ in New York is confused by conflicting rumours. It seems though, that he was only 15 when he wrote *Heroin*, by popular consensus the most harrowing song in pop. Later he became part

Left: Alvin Stardust: facetious machismo. *Above:* Dave Hill of Slade. The fact that even this ex-skinhead group introduced elements of camp into their stage costumes shows how pervasive camp had become in the pop scene of 1974.

The Sweet revived the mini opera format of the Shangri Las in hit singles like 'The Blockbusters' and 'Ballroom Blitz', which included sound effects and recitative.

Opposite: Elton John in concert. 'If we wish to succeed' said the eighteenth-century French novelist Crébillon fils, 'we must make ourselves preposterous'.

Above: The New York Dolls: America's more acerbic brand of camp rock. *Right:* Brian Eno was the most eyecatching member of Roxy Music when it first appeared in 1972. He later pursued a solo career which included composing music for Derek Jarman's film *Sebastiane*.

Freddie Mercury of the rock group Queen. Their repertoire includes such camp songs as 'Fat-bottomed Girls' and 'She Makes Me Storm Trooper in Stilettoes' as well as a hilarious version of Shirley Bassey's 'Hey Big Spender'.

of *The Exploding Plastic Inevitable*, a multi-media show incorporating films, a light show, music, and a whip dance performed by Gerard Malanga and Nico, a beautiful, blonde German girl who sang in a style reminiscent of Marlene Dietrich. The musicians in this 'happening' (Reed among them) began to perform on their own, calling themselves The Velvet Underground.

They sang about the decadent side of New York, about drugs, transvestites and prostitutes; 'Venus in Furs' was

Lou Reed: exemplary sleaze.

their sombre, doomladen tribute to Sacher (masochism) Masoch's novel. None of this material, recorded during the soggy days of Flower Power, was commercially successful, but it was highly influential in music circles, especially in Britain. From Andy Warhol via Lou Reed, the future stars of Glam Rock learnt their sense of style, their camp theatricality and their love of shocking people.

However, Lou Reed remained largely a cult figure unknown to the general public until 1972, when David Bowie produced his second solo album: *Transformer* and the single from it, 'Walk on the Wild Side', were number one hits on both sides of the Atlantic.

> Your face when sleeping is sublime,
> And then you open up your eyes.
> Then comes pancake Factor Number One,
> Eyeliner, rose-hips and lip-gloss are such fun.
> You're a slick little girl,
> You're a slick little girl.
> Rouge and colouring, incense and ice,
> Perfume and kisses, ooh it's all so nice.
> You're a slick little girl,
> You're a slick little girl.
>
> Now we're coming out,
> Out of our closets,
> Out on the streets,
> Yeah, we're coming out!

Opposite: Grace Jones.

When you're in bed it's so wonderful,
It'd be so nice to fall in love.
When you get dressed I really get my fill;
People say it's impossible.
Gowns lovely made out of lace,
And all the things that you do to your face,
You're a slick little girl,
You're a slick little girl.
Eye-liner, whitener, then colour the eyes
Yellow and green, ooh what a surprise!
You're a slick little girl,
You're a slick little girl.

Now we're coming out,
Out of our closets,
Out on the streets,
Yes, we're coming out!'

Adam Ant, one of the first pop stars to explore video fully. One production featured Diana Dors surrounded by four muscle men in a sequence reminiscent of Mae West's Las Vegas cabaret act.

Soft Cell: deliberate dinkiness.

Glam Rock's successors, Punk and Disco, carried on the camp tradition. Punk's outrageousness and eclectic clothing owe much to Marc Bolan and early Roxy Music, and, although they have been tempted by commercial success to make 'straight' pop songs, Blondie began as camp *pasticheurs* of pop in the Roxy Music mould. Village People, whose single, 'Y.M.C.A.', was the best-selling record of 1979, poked fun at the American ideal of manhood in a way parallel to Swinging London's parody of the stiff upper lip. Bryan Ferry's ex-girlfriend, Amanda Lear, has pursued the camp style he developed for her on the covers of his early albums to become Europe's most popular female singer. Among her rivals is Grace Jones, a singer with a great flair for publicity and as strapping a black woman as ever stalked the novels of Firbank and Van Vechten. In 1980, the arrival of the New Romantic movement signalled a new wave of art school rock music. The

A Dormeuil advertisement makes use of a titillating camp transvestism, against a background that apes art deco, one of the most popular of camp enthusiasms.

Opposite: American rock singer Wayne County—in a sex all of his own.

young gents who formed such groups as Ultravox, Soft Cell, Adam and the Ants and Japan have successfully revivified the Bowie/Ferry mode of applying collage techniques to music, lyrics, promotional material and clothes. The video boom has further increased the importance of visual self-presentation in pop.

With camp's pervasion of rock music, the process of democratisation is complete. Like fornication, camp is an irresponsible and slightly dangerous pleasure that is no longer the perogative of an economic elite, but the birth-right of all. Camp is enjoyed by artists, politicians, teeny

boppers and the millions of families who watch camp comedians on peak-time television. A week hardly goes by
without some camp figure (an interior decorator, perhaps,
or a stage designer) being featured on television arts programmes, in the Sunday supplements or in glossy magazines. Camp has become the dominant sensibility in picture
galleries, nightclubs and theatres. Many commentators
have noted how frivolous life has become. Camp, in its
various media, is a manifestation of this frivolity in the
sphere of culture.

John Inman in *Are You Being
Served*—a camp situation comedy set
in a department store. In the
background, Mollie Sugden as a
modern Lady Wishfort.

Man with monkey, London, 1980s.

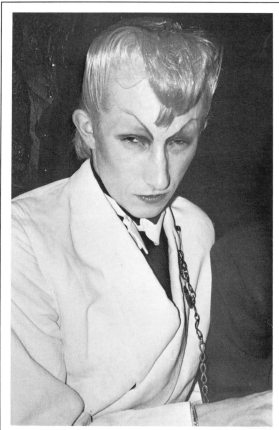

Celebration

Achievements. Qualities. Virtues. Delights.

Camp may be regarded as an experiment conducted over several centuries to find a mode of behaviour appropriate to the increasingly complex and sophisticated nature of urban life. It is an experiment that has engaged some brilliant minds, whose findings we have seen recorded in the arts.

It would be as well to recall, however, that camp is primarily a mode of behaviour and only secondarily a sensibility, that in contrast there is something introspective in all the arts—even the most off-the-cuff salon verses. To this extent, none of the arts can ever provide an accurate reflection of the truly camp.

Further, quintessentially camp people—the most original, the most amusing and the most influential—created very little in the arts themselves, though they inspired a great deal of creation by others. Beau Brummell, Robert de Montesquiou and Brian Howard did not write an important poem between them, but they did create a mode of behaviour, a style, a 'set', the description of which is so much of the attraction in the work of at least three major writers—Disraeli, Proust and Evelyn Waugh. The personalities of the first three men were at the very core of the latter three's success.

'Writing is a mechanic part of wit,' said Sir George Etherege, 'A gentleman should never go beyond a song or a billet.'

'It is the process of painting which is repellent,' echoed Max Beerbohm. 'To force from little tubes of lead a glutinous flamboyance and to defile, with the hair of camel therein steeped, taut canvas, is hardly the diversion of a gentleman.'

Brummell, Montesquiou and Howard, minor camp poets but major camp personalities, put into behaviour the impulses that might have gone into poetry. Wilde wrote:

'Good artists exist simply in what they make, and consequently are perfectly uninteresting in what they are. A great poet, a really good poet, is the most unpoetical of creatures. But inferior poets are absolutely fascinating. The worse their rhymes are, the more picturesque they look. The mere fact of having published a book of second-rate sonnets makes a man quite irresistible. He lives the poetry he cannot write. The others write the poetry they dare not realise.'

Artifice queening it once more: the rarified air of camp on London's streets in the 1980s.

Disraeli, Proust and Waugh had a trait of common sense, of sheer dreary doggedness that was lacking in the men who inspired them. Even Wilde only pretended to pretend. The effortless brilliance of successful camp writers (Disraeli claimed, 'When I want to read a book, I write one') is necessarily a fraud. Disraeli's and Wilde's plagiarisms, their cheating, their short cuts and their evasions should be seen as slight backslidings from a habit of hard work so disciplined that even the most pitiless of industrial task-masters, even the most beefy of burghers, would have been impressed.

Brummell, Montesquiou and Howard, on the other hand, had no sterner stuff in their souls. True ephemerids, they were lighter, more ethereal creatures. More fitted for flight than their imitators, they described a freer, much more spectacular trajectory in their brief escape from mundanity. Recklessly, they poured all their genius into the moment. They were, perhaps, men of genius but no talent.

The fact that they left so little personal testimony in the form of concrete artistic achievement should make us wonder all the more at the extent of their influence. Who is there among us who can say that he has never, intentionally or unintentionally, raised an eyebrow in the manner of Beau Brummell or stood posing a little after the style of Robert de Montesquiou? There is a quality in their charm that reaches us even over great distances in time. Camp is elusive but curiously powerful. The camp style in literature, film, music, the fine arts and fashion has become so familiar that we often even forget to think of it as camp; one of the reasons why camp is difficult to define is that it is no longer confined to cliques that the intellect can easily assimilate, but has entered into the behaviour of us all and affected our way of looking at things. Sometimes it is easy to overlook it, at others, society's margins seem to have expanded to cover the whole, and we may be teased by the notion that when social historians come to look back at our era, they may see it as an age not of existentialism or socialism or feminism, but of camp.

Not only has camp sensibility broadened, but the supply of trivia has expanded to meet that sensibility. When Pope's contemporary, John Gay, wrote his poem 'Trivia' ('Thou, Trivia, Goddess, aid my song') about a proto-*boulevardier* who strolled around the streets of London enjoying its trivia, he portrayed a connoisseur picking out odd details here and there, prizing them where he could find them—styles of coats or canes, the occasional troupe of street players, street cries and shops that 'lure the eye'. The poem would have to be very different if it were written today. To walk about Piccadilly or the Place Pigalle or Times Square is to be snowed under with trivia, to be confronted with a landscape of concentrated crassness. With its overcrowding, its straining after splendour, its fraudulent cheerfulness and its cod sophistication, the scene solicits the eye with gross commercial gestures, pours musical sedatives into the ear and goads the genitals with gratuitous sexual display. It has much in common with a female impersonator.

When a camp person walks through a modern city, he must feel that the configurations of that landscape are his own. The city is a veritable kaleidoscope of camp fads, lacking only the saving grace of self-mockery.

Society is more conducive to camp than ever. It is richer and more leisured, with more widespread claims to education. The cleavage between work and leisure is greater than ever before, so that camp has both more to defy and a greater arena of frivolity in which to frolic. Life is more thoroughly theatricalised, with fictional versions of reality available for individual consumption twenty-four hours a day through the media. More people are more bored—Regency dandies thought they were bored, but they were playing in the mere foothills of boredom.

There is more social mobility: the individual has a wider choice of roles and styles. Traditional sexual roles have been cheapened by the industrialisation of sex and discredited by feminism. Religious beliefs and moral values likely to oppose camp have been pushed back by the advance of blanket scepticism.

Nowadays, a crusading spirit of egalitarianism, underpinned by a less laudable distaste for the difficult, seeks to deny that there are any real differences of quality between highbrow and lowbrow culture. More and more people are being refreshingly unaffected in their choice of reading matter, refreshingly lacking in snobbery in their interior decoration, and refreshingly honest about their love of children's TV programmes. Millions upon millions are refreshingly ready to admit to their preference for silly old films, refreshingly brazen about wearing old-fashioned clothes and refreshingly forward in patronising bad taste generally. This exaltation of mediocrity is camp at its most sterile. More often than not, it is simply a matter of natural preferences disguised as condescension.

What then, have been the successes of the camp experiment? What can be said in its favour?

Total sincerity is a terrible thing. It is fierce, relentless and unable to relax. It cannot be easy-going or take things as they come. It leaves no latitude for humour. There is fanaticism in it. A totally sincere man is a limited man because, confined to one frame of reference, he lacks intellectual manoeuvrability, and because he is unable to comprehend his fellows, most of whom are insincere much of the time. There could even be something inhuman about him.

If it follows that we should be at least a little insincere, is it not better that our insincerity, rather than being secret and cankerous—of the sort that eventually deceives the person who harbours it—should be of the self-conscious, candid kind that we call camp? If we must be insincere, is it not better to be so cheerfully?

Although in some directions camp enjoys exaggeration (Wilde: 'Nothing succeeds like excess'), in others, it is a moderating influence. The camp never take themselves too seriously or stand on their dignity. Camp people do not start wars, or institute inquisitions or reigns of terror. Camp people are neither authoritarian, nor obsessive. Not having the allegiance or commitment to any system that would impart urgency or forcefulness to ideas, the camp person is free to regard them with a certain sardonic detachment, indeed to toy with them.

If camp people overestimate the value of appearance, it is only to the same extent as the rest of us underestimate it. They at least reject the deliberate, hieratic ugliness of the conventional male: they are not grey and anonymous, and they do not have the grey faults of pomposity and stultifying respectability. They decline to take refuge in the bogus decorum of maturity, and the specious dictates and presumptuous duties of middleclassness *oblige* do not interest them. If they play the fool, at least they do not do so in earnest. If their ideas of luxury are corny, they are still to be preferred to the inept luxury that the droopy-mouthed daughters of the bourgeoisie learn from television and glossy magazines. Camp people may, in the end, fail to be beautiful, witty and charming, but they do recognise these values by their attempts. Affectation implies appreciation of literary merit: in showing off, there must be companionability; in scandal-mongering, there must be a fascination with human affairs; in outrageousness there must be candour, and in frivolity there must be a love of fun.

Insincerity may not be exactly a virtue in itself, but, subject to proper checks, it may give rise to such good qualities as the desire to please, to entertain, to make something special of an occasion. At their best, the camp exhibit a largesse of spirit, a superabundant sweetness of temper, a quick-burgeoning gaiety. Nothing breeds as quickly as lies, and, perhaps because it is akin to lying, camp wit is quick, too. In certain circumstances, the limited nature of camp can be an advantage since excellence thrives within narrow limits: camp turns of wit are often of the finest: the best camp novels are among the very small number of which we can say that we should rather read them than have read them, and the best camp comedies are without equal. 'To read a good comedy' wrote Hazlitt, 'is to keep the best company in the world, where the best things are said and the most amusing happen. We would give our fingers to be able to talk so ourselves, or to hear others talk so. In turning over the pages of the best comedies we are almost transported into another world.' Good camp company transports that other world into ours, the ground beneath our feet becomes boards, and we find ourselves hearing others talk wittily and, perhaps, even hearing ourselves do so too: camp brings the realms of pure comedy down to earth and makes life lighter, brighter and more carefree.

It is in the nature of all ideologies to select certain aspects of life, to isolate them, and to proclaim them as the most significant—the aspects by which we should interpret and regulate our lives. Camp in its ideological dimension is no exception to this rule, but it is exceptional in choosing not to dwell, like other ideologies, upon life's tiresome or sordid aspects. Camp has annexed and civilised areas of delight that have otherwise hardly been explored. It has beaten tracks through jungles of enjoyment and made them accessible. It has reclaimed pleasures that today's more militant philosophies declare no longer viable.

It has cultivated, above all, the pleasures that assert themselves when life is not strictly goal-orientated: flirtation, dalliance, day-dreaming, banter and mockery—things that are difficult to fit into any sensible, systematic approach to life. When taken singly, they may seem insignificant, but taken in accumulation, they may, in their quiet way, form a large part of the finer things of life. Feminists may not relish the traditionally feminine pleasures of self-adornment, following fashion, buying things, vacillation, the decorative arts, hypochondria and gossip, but these things are nevertheless part of life, and the camp recognise them as such and make the most of them. Camp specialises in the pleasure of idleness—parties, parades and dancing; it is better organised in these matters than any of the rival ideologies. Happiness is notoriously difficult to quantify, but certainly no one observes its outward forms as closely as the camp.

Time and time again, in attempting to convey the experience of camp, we have invoked childhood. Versailles was called a toy by Walpole; sex as presented by Mae West subsides into a child's game, and the poetry of the Sitwells has a nursery rhyme quality. Camp bitchery has something of the cruelty of childhood, and camp histrionics can be childish. The simple, bold colours of camp are ice-cream colours: camp's favourite colour is pink: nursery pink, sugary pink, screaming pink. Camp keeps the faculty of wonder alive. It combines intellectual virtuosity with child-like freshness of vision. It sees through the many pompous pretences and dishonest compromises of the grown-up world. Maturity, it infers, must not be taken seriously.

'Experience is a fraud.' says the Spirit of Camp, 'Strive for innocence.'

Bibliography

Abse, Leo 'How to recognise tomorrow's spy' in *The Times*, London, 26th October 1981.

Ackroyd, Peter *Dressing Up: Transvestism and Drag, the History of an Obsession* Thames & Hudson 1979.

Acton, Harold *Memoirs of an Aesthete* Methuen 1948.

Acton, Harold *More Memoirs of an Aesthete* Methuen 1970.

Adam, Antoine *Grandeur and Illusion. French Literature and Society 1600-1715* translated by Herbert Tint. Weidenfeld & Nicolson 1972.

Anger, Kenneth *Hollywood Babylon* Dell, New York 1975.

Aretino: Selected Letters translated by George Bull. Penguin 1976.

Babuscio, Jack 'Camp and the gay sensibility' in *Gays and Film* ed. Richard Dyer. B.F.I. 1977.

Barthes, Roland *Wilhelm von Gloeden* Amelio Editore, Naples 1978.

Battersby, Martin 'Diaghilev's Influence on Fashion and Decoration' in *The World of Serge Diaghilev* by Charles Spencer and Philip Dyer. Paul Elek 1974.

Baudelaire, Charles *Intimate Journals* translated by Christopher Isherwood, 1930; reprinted by Methuen 1949; Panther 1969.

Baudelaire, Charles 'Le peintre de la vie moderne' in *Baudelaire: Oeuvres Complètes* Gallimard, Paris 1972.

Beardsley, Aubrey *The Story of Venus and Tannhäuser* 1907, reprinted Tandem 1967.

Beaton, Cecil *My Royal Past. By Baroness von Bülop as told to Cecil Beaton* Batsford 1939; Weidenfeld & Nicolson 1960.

Beaton, Cecil *The Wandering Years. Diaries 1922-1939* Weidenfeld & Nicolson 1961.

Beaton, Cecil *Self Portrait with Friends. The Selected Diaries of Cecil Beaton 1926-1974* ed. Richard Buckle. Weidenfeld & Nicolson 1979.

Beauvoir, Simone de *Le Deuxième Sexe* (1949) translated as *The Second Sex* by H.M. Parshley. Jonathan Cape 1953; Penguin 1967.

Beckford, William *Vathek* (1784) Everyman's Library Shorter Novels, vol. 3. J.M. Dent 1939.

Beerbohm, Max *The Works of Max Beerbohm* Bodley Head 1896.

Beerbohm, Max *Zuleika Dobson* Heinemann 1911; Penguin 1952.

Benkowitz, Miriam J. *Ronald Firbank. A Biography* Weidenfeld & Nicolson 1969.

Benson, E.F. *Queen Lucia* Hutchinson 1920; Corgi 1979.

Benson, E.F. *Miss Mapp* Hutchinson 1922; Corgi 1979.

Bernhardt, Sarah *Memoirs of Sarah Bernhardt* translated by Sandy Lesberg. Peebles Press, New York 1977.

Betjeman, John *Mount Zion* James Press 1931. Also in *John Betjeman's Collected Poems* John Murray 1970.

Blake, Robert *Disraeli* Eyre & Spottiswoode 1966.

Blunt, Anthony *Art and Architecture in France 1500-1700* Penguin 1953.

Blunt, Wilfred *The Dream King: Ludwig II of Bavaria* Hamish Hamilton 1970.

Boyle, Andrew *The Climate of Treason* Hutchinson 1979, Coronet (revised edition) 1980.

Brophy, Brigid *Beardsley and his World* Thames & Hudson 1976.

Brown, Curtis F. *American Kitsch* Universe Books, New York 1975.

Bryden, Ronald 'The Spies Who Came Into Camp' in an *Observer* colour magazine, August 1966.

Burns, Elizabeth *Theatricality* Longman 1972.

Capote, Truman *The dogs bark. Public people and private places* Random House 1973; Weidenfeld & Nicolson 1974.

Capote, Truman *Breakfast at Tiffany's* Hamish Hamilton 1958; Penguin 1961.

Carlyle, Thomas *Sartor Resartus* James Fraser 1841; J.M. Dent 1908.

Carter, Angela 'Notes for a theory of 'sixties style' *New Society* 1967. Also in *Arts and Society* ed. Paul Barker. Fontana 1977.

Castellane, Boni de *Confessions of the Marquis de Castellane* Thornton Butterworth 1924.

Castiglione, Baldassare *The Courtier* (1528) transl. George Bull. Penguin 1967.

Cellini, Benvenuto *Autobiography* (1571) transl. George Bull. Penguin 1956.

Chambers, Sir William 'Designs for Chinese Buildings, Furniture, Dresses, Machines and Utensils' collected in *A Documentary History of Art* ed. Elizabeth G. Holt. Doubleday Anchor Books, New York 1958.

Chapman, Guy *Beckford* Jonathan Cape 1937.

Chastel, André *Italian Art* transl. Peter and Linda Murray. Faber & Faber 1972.

Chesterfield, Lord *Letters to his son and others* (1774) Everyman's Library, J.M. Dent 1929.

Choisy, Abbé de *The Transvestite Memoirs of the Abbé de Choisy and The Story of the Marquise/Marquis de Banneville* transl. R.H.F. Scott. Peter Owen 1973.

Cibber, Colley *Love's Last Shift* (1696) collected in *Restoration Comedy* vol. 3 ed. A. Norman Jeffares. Folio Press 1974.

Cohn, Nik *I Am Still the Greatest Says Johnny Angelo* Secker & Warburg 1967; Penguin 1970.

Cohn, Nik *Wop-bop-a-loo-bop-lop-bam-boom. Pop from the beginning* Weidenfeld & Nicolson 1969; Paladin 1970.

Cole, Hubert *Brummell* Hart-Davis MacGibbon 1977.

Congreve, William *The Way of the World* (1700) collected in *Restoration Plays* J.M. Dent 1976.

Connely, Willard *The Reign of Beau Brummell* Cassell 1940.

Connolly, Cyril *The Enemies of Promise* Routledge 1938; André Deutsch 1973.

Connolly, Cyril 'Where Engels Fears to Tread' (1936-37) collected in *The Condemned Playground. Essays 1927-44* Routledge 1945.

Coward, Noel *The Vortex* in *Contemporary British Dramatists*, Vol. 29, Ernest Benn 1924, and in *Master Playwrights*, Eyre Methuen 1979.

Crébillon fils *The Wayward Head and Heart* (1736-38) transl. Barbara Bray, Oxford University Press 1963.

Cruse, Amy *An Englishman and his Books in the Early Nineteenth Century* Harrap 1930.

Diderot, Denis *Rameau's Nephew* 1761; transl. Leonard Tancock, Penguin 1966.

Disraeli, Benjamin *Vivian Grey* Henry Colburn 1826; John Lane the Bodley Head 1906.

Disraeli, Benjamin *Sybil* (1845) in The World's Classics series, Oxford University Press 1926.

Driberg, Tom *Guy Burgess: a Portrait with Background* Weidenfeld & Nicolson 1956.

Ellis, Havelock *Psychology of Sex* Heinemann Medical Books Ltd 1933, Pan Piper 1959.

Etherege, Sir George *The Man of Mode* (1676) in *Restoration Plays* J.M. Dent 1976.

Farquhar, George *The Beaux' Stratagem* (1707) in *Restoration Plays* J.M. Dent 1976.

Firbank, Ronald *Inclinations* Grant Richards 1916, Duckworth 1929.

Firbank, Ronald *Valmouth* Grant Richards 1919, Penguin 1961.

Firbank, Ronald *The Flower Beneath the Foot* Grant Richards 1923, Duckworth 1929.

Firbank, Ronald *Concerning the Eccentricities of Cardinal Pirelli* Grant Richards 1926, Penguin 1961.

Freud, Sigmund *On Sexuality* The Pelican Freud Library, vol. 7 1977.

Friedan, Betty *The Feminine Mystique* Victor Gollancz 1963, Penguin 1965.

Gautier, Théophile *Mademoiselle de Maupin* (1835) transl. Joanna Richardson, Penguin 1981.

Gautier, Théophile *Le Capitaine Fracasse* (1863) Librairie Illustrée, Paris 1900.

Gay, John 'Trivia' (1716) and 'To a Lady on her Passion for Old China' (1725) in *John Gay. Poetry and Prose* Oxford University Press 1974.

Genet, Jean *Notre Dame des Fleurs* L'Arbalète, Lyons 1943; revised Librarie Gallimard, Paris 1951. Transl. Bernard Frechtman, Anthony Blond 1964; Panther 1966.

Genet, Jean *Journal du Voleur* (1949) transl. Bernard Frechtman, Anthony Blond 1965, Penguin 1967.

Gibbon, Edward *The History of the Decline and Fall of the Roman Empire* (1776-88) J.M. Dent 1954.

Gidal, Peter *Andy Warhol. Films and Painting* Studio Vista 1971.

Green, Martin *Children of the Sun. A narrative of 'decadence' in England after 1918* Constable 1977.

Greer, Germaine *The Female Eunuch* MacGibbon & Kee 1970, Paladin 1971.

Harland, Henry *The Cardinal's Snuff Box* John Lane 1900; Nelson 1914.

Harland, Henry *My Friend Prospero* John Lane 1904, Penguin 1947.

Hazlitt, William 'Wit and Humour', 'English Comedy' and 'Vivian Grey and the Dandy School' collected in *William Hazlitt. Essayist and Critic* Frederick Warne 1889.

Hebdige, Dick *Subculture: the meaning of style* Methuen 1981.

Herodian in two volumes with an English translation by C.R. Whittaker Heinemann 1969.·

Hess, Thomas B. 'J'accuse Marcel Duchamp' in *Art News* LXIII no. 10; collected in *Marcel Duchamp in Perspective* ed. Joseph Masheck. Prentice Hall, Englewood Cliffs, New Jersey 1975.

Hoggart, Richard *The Uses of Literacy* Chatto & Windus 1957, Pelican 1958.

Holland, Norman H. *The First Modern Comedies* Harvard University Press 1959.

Holland, Vyvyan 'Ronald Firbank: A Memoir' collected in *Ronald Firbank, Memoirs and Critiques* ed. Mervyn Horder. Duckworth 1977.

Howard, Brian 'Baroness Ada' collected in *Brian Howard. Portrait of a Failure* Anthony Blond 1968.

Howard, Philip *New Words for Old* Hamish Hamilton 1977.

Huxley, Aldous *Antic Hay* Chatto & Windus 1923, Penguin Books 1948.

Isherwood, Christopher *Goodbye to Berlin* The Hogarth Press 1939, Triad/Granada 1977.

Isherwood, Christopher *The World in the Evening* Methuen 1954, Avon Books 1978.

Jackson, Holbrook *The Eighteen Nineties* Grant Richards 1913, Pelican 1939.

Janeway, Elizabeth *Man's World, Woman's Place. A Study in Social Mythology* Michael Joseph 1972.

Jares, Joe *Whatever Happened to Gorgeous George?* Tempo Books, Grosset & Dunlap, New York 1944.

Jullian, Philippe *Dreamers of Decadence: symbolist paintings of the 1890s* transl. Robert Baldick. Pall Mall Press 1971, Phaidon 1974.

Jullian, Philippe *Robert de Montesquiou: A Fin de Siècle Prince* transl. John Haylock and Francis King. Secker & Warburg 1967.

Kleinberg, Seymour ed. *The Other Persuasion* Random House New York 1977, Pan 1978.

La Bruyère, Jean de *Characters* (1688) transl. Jean Stewart, Penguin 1970.

Lafayette, Madame de *La Princesse de Clèves* (1678) transl. Nancy Mitford, Euphorion Books 1956; Penguin 1962 (revised).

Lahr, John *Prick Up Your Ears. The Biography of Joe Orton* Allen Lane 1978.

Laing, R.D. *The Divided Self* Tavistock Publications 1960, Pelican 1965.

Lambert, Constant *Music Ho! A Study of Music in Decline* Faber & Faber 1934, Penguin Books 1948.

Lancaster, Marie Jaqueline *Brian Howard. Portrait of a Failure* Anthony Blond 1968.

Laver, James *Dandies* Weidenfeld and Nicolson 1968.

Lehmann, John *A Nest of Tigers. Edith, Osbert and Sacheverell Sitwell in their Times* Macmillan 1968.

Lister, Thomas *Granby* (1826) The Modern Novelists in 50 Volumes. Colburn's Modern Standard Novelists, vol. II. 1839.

Lough, John *An Introduction to Seventeenth Century France* Longmans, Green 1954.

Lucie-Smith, Edward *Concise History of French Painting* Thames & Hudson 1971.

Lytton, Bulwer *Pelham, or the Adventures of a Gentleman* (1828), also in Colburn's Modern Standard Novelists vol. II 1839.

Marshall, Arthur 'A Schoolgirl Story' in *1st Chance* October 1952.

Melly, George *Revolt into Style* Allen Lane 1970.

Millet, Kate *Sexual Politics* Rupert Hart-Davis 1971, Virago 1977.

Mitford, Nancy *The Sun King* Hamish Hamilton 1966.

Mitford, Nancy *Love in a Cold Climate* Hamish Hamilton 1945.

Moers, Ellen *The Dandy, Brummell to Beerbohm* Secker & Warburg 1960.

Molière, Jean-Baptiste Poquelin *Les Précieuses Ridicules* (1659), *L'Impromptu de Versailles* (1663), *Le Bourgeois Gentilhomme* (1670), *Les Fourberies de Scapin* (1671), collected in *The Plays of Molière* in French with an English Translation and Notes by A.R. Waller vols, II, III and VII, John Grant 1926.

Nuttall, Jeff *Bomb Culture* MacGibbon & Kee 1968, Paladin 1970.

O'Donnell, Peter *Modesty Blaise* Souvenir Press 1965; Pan 1966.

Orton, Joe *Entertaining Mr Sloane* Hamish Hamilton 1964, Eyre Methuen 1973.

Orton, Joe *Loot* Methuen 1967.

Orton, Joe *Up Against It* Eyre Methuen 1979.

Orwell, George 'Good Bad Books' (1945) in *The Collected Essays, Journalism and Letters of George Orwell* Vol. 4. Secker & Warburg 1968.

Osborne, John *A Patriot for Me* Faber & Faber 1966.

Pascal, Blaise *Pensées* transl. A.J. Krailsheimer, Penguin 1966.

Peacock, Thomas Love *Nightmare Abbey* (1818), collected in vol. LVII of Bentley's Standard Novels, 1837.

Pearson, Hesketh *The Life of Oscar Wilde* Methuen 1946.

Pepys, Samuel *The Diaries of Samuel Pepys. A New and Complete Transcription* ed. Robert Latham and William Matthews.

Petronius *The Satyricon* transl. J.P. Sullivan; Penguin 1965.

Pope, Alexander *The Rape of the Lock* (1714) in *Pope. The Rape of the Lock and other Poems* Blackwood's English Classics, William Blackwood 1901.

Proust, Marcel *A La Recherche du Temps Perdu* (1913-27) transl. C.K. Scott-Moncrieff and A. Mayer and published by Chatto & Windus as *Remembrance of Things Past* 1922-31.

Rees, Goronwy Rees *A Chapter of Accidents* Chatto & Windus 1977.

Rochefoucauld, Duc de la *The Maxims of the Duc de la Rochefoucauld* transl. Constantine FitzGibbon; Allan Wingate 1957.

Rolfe, Frederick *Hadrian the Seventh* Chatto & Windus 1904, Penguin 1963.

Rolfe, Frederick *Don Tarquinio* Chatto & Windus 1905.

Rolfe, Frederick *Hubert's Arthur* Cassell 1935.

Saint-Simon at Versailles ed. and transl. by Lucy Norton; Hamish Hamilton 1958.

Saki *The Unbearable Bassington* (1912) and *The Story-Teller* (1914) collected in *The Complete Works of Saki* The Bodley Head 1980.

Sansovino, Francesco *Tenth Day, Novella VII* in *The Italian Novelists* transl. Thomas Roscoe 1825. The Chandos Classics, Frederick Warne 1868.

Sévigné, Madame de *Madame de Sévigné. Her letters and her world* transl. Arthur Stanley; Eyre & Spottiswoode 1946.

Shearman, John *Mannerism* Penguin 1967.

Sitwell, Edith *Façade and Other Poems* Gerald Duckworth 1950.

Sitwell, Sir Osbert *Laughter in the Next Room* Macmillan 1949.

Skinner, Cornelia Otis *Elegant Wits and Grand Horizontals* The Riverside Press, Cambridge 1962.

Sontag, Susan 'Notes on Camp' in *Partisan Review* XXXI. 4 1964.

Sprigge, Elizabeth and Kihm, Jean-Jacques *Jean Cocteau: the Man and the Mirror* Gollancz 1968.

Storr, Anthony *The Integrity of the Personality* Heinemann Medical Books 1960, Pelican 1963.

Storr, Anthony *Sexual Deviation* Penguin 1964.

Sternberg, Jacques *Kitsch* Editions Planète, Paris 1971, Academy Editions 1972.

Stoller, Robert J. *Perversion. The Erotic Form of Hatred* Harvester Press Ltd 1976, Quartet 1977.

Suetonius *The Twelve Caesars* transl. Robert Graves, Penguin 1957.

Swinburne, Algernon Charles 'Dolores' in *The Complete Works of Algernon Charles Swinburne. Poetical Works, vol. I* Heinemann 1925.

Thompson, Michael 'An Anatomy of Rubbish' New Society 1969, collected in *Arts in Society* ed. Paul Barker, Fontana 1977.

Tolson, Andrew *The Limits of Masculinity* Tavistock Publications 1977.

Took, Barry and Feldman, Marty *The Bona Book of Julian and Sandy* Robson Books 1976.

Trilling, Lionel *Sincerity and Authenticity* Harvard University Press 1972.

Tuska, Jon *The Films of Mae West* Citadel Press, Secaucus, New Jersey 1973.

Tyler, Parker *Underground Film: a critical history* Secker & Warburg 1971.

Vanbrugh, Sir John *The Relapse* (1697) in *Restoration Comedy, vol. III* ed. A. Norman Jeffares, Folio Press 1974.

Vanbrugh, Sir John *The Provok'd Wife* (1697) in *Restoration Plays* J.M. Dent 1976.

Vasari's Lives of the Artists ed. Betty Burroughs, Allen & Unwin 1960.

Vechten, Carl Van *Peter Whiffle: his life and works* Alfred A. Knopf, New York 1922.

Vechten, Carl Van *The Blind Bow Boy* Alfred A. Knopf, New York 1923.

Vechten, Carl Van *The Tattooed Countess* Alfred A. Knopf, New York 1924.

Vidal, Gore *Myra Breckinridge* Little, Brown Boston 1968, Anthony Blond 1968.

Voiture, Vincent in *The Penguin Book of French Verse, Vol 2, 16th-18th centuries* Penguin Poets 1958.

Voltaire *The Age of Louis XIV* transl. Martyn P. Pollock, J.M. Dent 1926.

Walpole, Horace *Letters of Horace Walpole* J.M. Dent 1926.

Ward, Plumer *Tremaine* Henry Colburn 1825.

Warhol, Andy *The Philosophy of Andy Warhol—From A to B and Back Again* Michael Dempsey/Cassell 1975.

Andy Warhol's Exposures ed. Bob Colacello, Hutchinson 1979.

Waugh, Evelyn *Put Out More Flags* Chapman & Hall 1942, Penguin 1943.

Waugh, Evelyn *Brideshead Revisited* Chapman & Hall 1945, Penguin 1951.

Whistler, James Abbott McNeill *The Gentle Art of Making Enemies* Heinemann 1890, Dover 1967.

Wilde, Oscar *The Picture of Dorian Gray* Lippincott's Magazine 1890, Oxford University Press 1974.

Wilde, Oscar *Intentions. The Decay of Lying—Pen, Pencil and Poison—The Critic as Artist—The Truth of Masks* James R. Osgood, McIlvaine 1891; Methuen 1908.

Wilde, Oscar *Lady Windermere's Fan* (1892), *A Woman of No Importance* (1893), *An Ideal Husband* (1895), *The Importance of Being Earnest* (1895), collected in *Complete Works of Oscar Wilde* Collins 1948.

Wilson, Angus *Hemlock and After* Secker & Warburg 1952.

Wolfe, Tom *The Kandy-Kolored Tangerine-Flake Streamline Baby* Jonathan Cape 1966.

Wolfe, Tom *Radical Chic and Mau-Mauing the Flak Catchers* Farrar Strauss, New York 1970.

Wood, Michael 'You can't go home again' *New Society* 1974. Collected in *Arts in Society* ed. Paul Barker, Fontana 1977.

Wycherley, William *The Complete Works of William Wycherley* ed. Montague Summers, Nonesuch Press 1924.

York, Peter *Style Wars* Sidgwick & Jackson 1980.

Acknowledgements

While every attempt has been made to trace holders of copyright in material reproduced in this book, this has not always been possible. Cameron Books therefore offers its apologies to any person or organisation to whom it has failed to give the appropriate acknowledgement.

Material from books appears by courtesy of the publishers, who are listed in the bibliography.

Song lyrics reproduced by kind permission of the following:

'Past, Present and Future' by Art Butler, Jerry Leiber and Mike Stoller. Copyright Leiber Stoller Songs Limited.

'Dedicated Follower of Fashion' by Ray Davies. Copyright Davray Music Ltd/Carlin Music Corporation.

'In Every Dream Home A Heartache' by Bryan Ferry. Copyright 1973 E.G. Music Limited.

'Remember Me' by V. Ashford & N. Simpson. Copyright Jobete Music (UK) Limited.

'Make Up' by Lou Reed. Copyright Warlock Music Ltd.

Pictures are reproduced by courtesy of the following:

Susan Adler 127 left
David Bailey 43
David Bailey for Ritz magazine 77
BBC 60, 62, 176
BBC Hulton Picture Library 15 top right, 24 right, 25 left, 38, 41 left, 64 bottom, 68 top, 78, 91, 93 right, 97, 137 top
Adrian Boot 144
British Museum, London 129
Photographie Bulloz 35
Paul Cox/L.F.I. 172, 173
Zoë Dominic 24 left, 53, 109
Mary Evans Picture Library 19, 37, 56
Fogg Art Museum, Harvard University, Grenville L. Winthrop Bequest 102
Foto Fiorentini 47
Richard Gollner: Radala Ass. 85 right
Frank Griffin L.F.I. 143 bottom
Angelo Hornak 20, 140
ITC 82
King's College Library, Cambridge 142 right
Lichtbildwerkstätte 'Alpenland' 132 left
London Features International 169 bottom
Mainline Pictures 127 right
Robyn Mandell, Chicago 163, 165 right, 167
The Raymond Mander and Joe Mitchenson Theatre Collection 16 right, 17 right, 21 bottom, 85 left, 90, 96, 131 top
Iain McKell 161
Milwaukee Art Museum Collection, Gift of the Women's Exchange 34

Alec Murray for Dormeuil 175
National Film Archive 2/3, 8 left & right, 12, 13 top & bottom, 14, 15 top left & bottom, 16 left, 17 right, 22 top, 54, 55 left, 59, 68 bottom, 75, 76 left & right, 86, 88, 89, 105 left & right, 124, 127 right, 128, 134, 135, 136 left & right, 139, 146, 147, 148 top and bottom left & right 149 top and bottom left & right, 154, 155 bottom
National Gallery of Art, Washington, Rosenwald Collection 58
National Portrait Gallery, London 100
Barry Plummer 145 left, 166 right & bottom
Popperfoto 55 right, 63, 92, 112, 159, 170
Jean-Marc Prouveur 107
Steve Rapport/L.F.I. 168
RCA 132 centre, 171
David Redfern Photography 98, 160, 169 top
David Redfern Photography/David Ellis 166 top left
Rex Features 145 left, 155 top, 156 left & right, 158, 164, 166 right & bottom
Derek W. Ridgers 177, 178
Mick Rock 113, 174
Scala/Firenze 48, 66
Sotheby's Belgravia (Cecil Beaton photographs) 18, 23, 31, 65, 69, 126, 133, 137 bottom, 142 left, 145 right
S.P.A.D.E.M. 138, 150
Charles Spencer Theatre Gallery 142
Syndication International 132 right
The Tate Gallery, London 22 bottom, 93 left, 153, 157
James Wedge 101

Index